Right Living
in a World Gone Wrong

David Allan Hubbard

InterVarsity Press
Downers Grove
Illinois 60515

© 1981 by Inter-Varsity Christian Fellowship of the United States of America

All rights reserved. No part of this book may be reproduced in any form without written permission from InterVarsity Press, Downers Grove, Illinois.

InterVarsity Press is the book-publishing division of Inter-Varsity Christian Fellowship, a student movement active on campus at hundreds of universities, colleges and schools of nursing. For information about local and regional activities, write IVCF, 233 Langdon St., Madison, WI 53703.

Distributed in Canada through InterVarsity Press, 1875 Leslie St., Unit 10, Don Mills, Ontario M3B 2M5, Canada.

ISBN 0-87784-470-4

Printed in the United States of America

Library of Congress Cataloging in Publication Data

Hubbard, David Allan.
  Right living in a world gone wrong.

  Includes bibliographies.
  1. United States—Moral conditions. 2. Sexual
ethics. 3. Christian ethics. 4. Church and social
problems—United States. I. Title.
HN90.M6H8   261.8'3   80-39671
ISBN 0-87784-470-4

15	14	13	12	11	10	9	8	7	6	5	4	3	2	1
93	92	91	90	89	88	87	86	85	84	83	82	81		

Introduction 7

1
Premarital Sex:
Why Wait When We Love Each Other? *11*

2
Homosexuality:
Why Can't I Love the Way I Want? *19*

3
Abortion:
It's My Body, Isn't It? *29*

4
Pornography:
It Won't Harm Me, Will It? *39*

5
Women's Rights:
Why Can't I Be Treated As a Person? *47*

6
Capital Punishment:
Isn't Killing Always Wrong? *55*

7
Euthanasia:
When Is Enough Enough? 65

8
Civil Disobedience:
What If the Law Seems Wrong? 75

9
Ecology:
How Careful Should We Be of Our Environment? 83

10
Consumerism:
How Can I Get My Money's Worth? 91

11
Affluence:
Why Can't I Spend What's Mine? 101

Conclusion *109*

Introduction

The appraisal of life in the days of the judges does not miss the modern mark by far: "In those days there was no king in Israel; every man did what was right in his own eyes" (Judg. 21:25). Nor has the current moral confusion left the people of Christ unscathed. The light of the world sputters half-dimmed in a shortage of ethical energy; the salt of the earth finds its tang sapped by accommodation to tasteless values; the city on the hill is all but obscured by smog partly of its own making.

We may ask self-righteously, "Who, me?" but we

have been all but swamped by a *secular* morality. Our skill at rationalizing has far outstripped our heart for discipline. The apostle Paul's plea for transformation wrought by a renewed mind that responds to divine mercy (Rom. 12:1-2) has been greeted by a shrug. We are alert to social trends yet indifferent to the implications of our Christian theology. We have rightly rejected the rigors of a legalism that gauges righteousness with the graphed precision of a Dow Jones average. But we have declined to develop a moral, social and political responsibility that is thoroughly Christian. Where we have not seized the throne ourselves, we have fawned as vassals in the courts of secularity.

If our morality has not been secular, it has often been *selective*. By inclination or training we have become much more sensitive to some biblical issues than to others. For example, consider the response to the broadcast of these chapters on "The Joyful Sound" radio program. We printed the talks in booklets of three or four each and offered them free to listeners. The first booklet containing the sexual themes—premarital sex, homosexuality, abortion and pornography—drew ten times more requests than did the booklet on consumerism, affluence and ecology.

I am not suggesting that evangelicals are the only Christians who selectively treasure some aspects of biblical morality above other aspects. Other wings of the church do the same, though their moral priorities may be political and social rather than personal or sexual. We are willing courtiers until the claims of God's kingship turn uncomfortable. Then we snatch the scepter from him.

We need to replace our secular or selective understandings of Christian life with one that can best be called *saintly*. The term may sound quaint, but we must not be put off by it. Saintly morality does not mean living righteously so that God and others will deem us saints. It means living righteously in all of our human responsibilities because God has already deemed us saints. He has called us to his love and grace and declared us righteous because of what Jesus Christ has done on our behalf in his life, death and resurrection.

We do not strive to be saints by practicing morality; we seek to live morally because in God's eyes—and what else ultimately counts?—we are already saints. Our saintly morality, then, gives us the perspective to deal with the dilemmas that threaten to tear us apart with ethical tensions. We find our guidelines neither in ethical abstractions about life's highest good nor in statistical considerations of social trends.

God's calling us to himself in Jesus Christ becomes the dominant ethical reality of our lives. If God's title for us is saints, our title for him is Lord. That relationship—our sainthood and God's lordship—is unyieldingly authoritarian. He, the One utterly holy, has called us holy and has set the terms of that holiness. Who God is, how he works, what he wants—these fix the moral boundaries within which we comport ourselves as saints. What is right in our own eyes becomes virtually irrelevant. Instead, we recognize that presiding over every area of life—personal, social, political, intellectual, vocational and recreational—is the true and living God.

That recognition may not give us every specific answer as we resist impalement on the horns of the dilemmas that vie to trap us. But assuredly, without that recognition, our morality will be impotent beyond description.

This book has one aim: to alert us to the theological realities that must govern our moral choices. To face all of life in the light of a living, loving, empowering and judging king is the beginning of Christian morality. In each chapter I have tried to sketch the way that such living helps us cope with the confusion of our day.

Thanks are due to my Fuller colleague Lewis Smedes. He graciously encouraged me to venture into print with these chapters whose subjects lie much more within his field of competence than mine. My gratitude goes also to my wife, Ruth, who edited and typed the book from my scribbled pages. Her counsel and support in this endeavor, as through the thirty-one years of our marriage, have been indispensable.

1

Premarital Sex:

Why Wait When We Love Each Other?

WHY SHOULD WE WAIT when we love each other? That question, in one form or another, is posed annually in thousands of homes and hundreds of pastors' studies across our land. The incidence of the question and the volume with which it is raised seem to be increasing.

Much in our society has conspired to make this happen. Sex, including promiscuous sex, is openly discussed and portrayed in the printed page and the electronic media. Subjects that once were whispered among intimates are now blazoned in headlines and broadcast throughout the land. Modern technology has furnished protection against disease and conception. Penicillin and the pill block many of the fears that served to inhibit premarital relations. The automobile—especially the camper and the van—together with singles' apartments have provided a seclusion that other generations might have longed for but did not experience.

Media, medicine and transportation may have contributed to the increased number of couples living together without formal marriage, but they do not provide the full explanation. If I had to isolate a single factor, I would select the breakdown in regard for the authority of the Hebrew-Christian view of marriage. Social pressures are undoubtedly strong: "everyone else is doing it, so it can't be all wrong." People lack the inner resolve, the heartfelt conviction, of what is right and what is wrong.

Marriage, to many moderns, is mere social custom, varying in usefulness from culture to culture and generation to generation. There is nothing God-given about it. It is subject to human change like hair styles or diet fads.

All of this presents Christians with a dilemma. Romantic affection and biological urges spur us to sexual experimentation, which our biblical heritage has deemed wrong. To practice complete restraint puts us at odds with our bodies and our friends; to engage in premarital sex sets us in conflict with Christian tradition.

The prolonged adolescence which modern life produces has only compounded the dilemma for young believers. The need for formal education in large doses and for a measure of financial independence before marriage has caused our generation to raise the average age at which young people, especially women, marry.

We all need help in dealing with the tensions of this dilemma. More than opinions or statistics or testimonials, we need a word from God. Nothing less than a fresh look at the Bible will help us to keep a sound perspective on sex amid all the confusion.

The Biblical Purposes of Sex

A biblical understanding of human sexuality begins with creation: "So God created man in his own image, in the image of God he created him; male and female he created them" (Gen. 1:27). Our sexuality—maleness and femaleness—is part of our heritage from the creative hand of God. The organs of reproduction and excitement, the glands that secrete male and female hormones, the nervous system that thrills to an affectionate touch—these are all gifts of God. Like all the Creator's works they have divinely ordered purposes to fulfill.

Enjoyment is surely one of their purposes. Why else would God have designed our minds and bodies to find such exquisite pleasure, such exhilarating excitement, such profound contentment in our lovemaking? We tingle, glow and thrill because God made us that way. If confirmation is needed of God's plan for our sexual enjoyment, we can certainly find it in the Song of Solomon whose pages are lighted with the joys of love:

As an apple tree among the trees of the wood,
so is my beloved among young men.
With great delight I sat in his shadow,
and his fruit was sweet to my taste. . . .

O that his left hand were under my head,
and that his right hand embraced me! (Song 2:3, 6)

How good of God to include descriptions of love's pleasures in his holy Book! Sex is for enjoyment. That was one of God's high purposes in making us male and female in his image.

Procreation is another of God's purposes to be fulfilled in our sexuality: "And God blessed them, and God said to them, 'Be fruitful and multiply, and fill the earth and subdue it; and have dominion over the fish of the sea and over the birds of the air and over every living thing that moves upon the earth' " (Gen. 1:28). God's plan was not simply for a human pair who would know him and love each other; it was for a whole human family. The man and the woman were given the urge and the power to reproduce so that God's purposes would be fulfilled: (1) the earth would be properly tended to and regulated and (2) God's name would be honored and glorified.

This latter purpose is key because human procreation is not merely a matter of survival, a natural process geared to keep the race from extinction. It is a holy participation in the universal task of making God's name known so that the whole creation will sound his praises. Human reproduction, therefore, is sacred and serious.

Enjoyment and procreation, then, are two of God's reasons for making us sexual beings. His most important purpose for sex, however, is *covenant*. Loyal, steadfast, caring, permanent relationships are what life, on God's terms, is all about. Father, Son and Holy Spirit exist eternally in the relationship of the Godhead. God lives in binding fellowship from eternity to eternity. Because he created us in his image we have a capacity for fellowship like God's. We were made to love and honor God and one another.

The picture of covenant is developed throughout the Bible. God's desire for fellowship and his knowledge that fellowship is the key to human life express themselves in a covenant that he made with Israel, his people. As the prophets, especially Hosea, noted, God took Israel as a wife to love and to cherish. Despite all her failings and wanderings, her rebellion and unfaithfulness, God loved her and kept her for his own.

In the New Testament, Paul used the concept of covenant to describe the relationship between Christ and his church: "Even so husbands should love their wives as their own bodies. He who loves his wife loves himself. For no man ever hates his own flesh, but nourishes and cherishes it, as Christ does the church, because we are members of his body. 'For this reason a man shall leave his father and mother and be joined to his wife, and the two shall become one flesh' " (Eph. 5:28-31). This passage explains covenant oneness which leads to covenant love. Christ's oneness with his people and his care for them become the model of Christian love and marriage.

In short, sexual relations were designed to be an expression, a demonstration, of the covenant love that God has for us his people. The permanence and the loyalty and the whole-souled commitment that God has shown us in Christ are to set the terms for our love.

No other setting but marriage can do this. Why wait when we love each other? The question is poignant and pressing when put by starry-eyed, warm-blooded people. Why wait? Because sex is for covenant, and covenant is both permanent and total.

The Practical Side

But if we love each other and share that commitment can we not proceed to full embracing before marriage? The question should not be ignored, if only because so many people are raising it.

Let us go back to the three biblical purposes of sex: enjoyment, procreation and covenant. *Enjoyment* in sex is a gift of God, but not a gift with which to tamper. Enjoyment, as God designed it, should have several ingredients: (1) it should be as free from fear and guilt as possible; (2) it should be a total emotional, spiritual and intellectual relationship as well as a physical delight; (3) it should serve to tie people more closely together in love, not to drive them apart. What setting best provides the ingredients that full enjoyment needs? The answer is not hard. Marriage alone provides security from fear of being used, seduced and abandoned; marriage alone gives opportunity for the total relationship in which true enjoyment flourishes.

Procreation is both a delight and duty given us by God. I do not mean that all families must have as many children as possible. Indeed, there may be cases where a couple should not have children of their own. But ordinarily sex and procreation do have a close connection because procreation is a possibility in any sexual relationship. No readily available method of contraception is foolproof. When a couple engages in intercourse, they must be prepared to accept the possibility and the responsibility of childbirth.

What setting best furnishes the context for that, especially the context that encourages a child to grow up to know and love God, which is procreation's central aim? Abortion, illegitimacy, forced matrimony—none of these is as responsible and as effective a way to obey God's will for our sexuality as marriage freely chosen.

Covenant is the decisive reason for waiting. Sexual intercourse is a badge and seal of a permanent covenant commitment. How do we know that we mean this commitment until we make it, and make it in a form that is hard to back away from? Is there not a basic danger in enjoying covenant intimacy without covenant commitment? Do not couples cause undue difficulties for themselves when they enjoy full privileges without full responsibilities? What do they then gain from the marriage ceremony? Only added emotional and financial burdens without equivalent privilege.

Why not just live together? Why marry at all? These questions deserve a more thorough answer than is possible here. We can start by saying that marriage is a well-proven way of demonstrating that we take the covenant of sex with great seriousness. We seal it with a public vow that makes it hard to break. We treat it like a contract so that we will be reminded in the difficult days of the importance of our obligation.

Beyond that, public marriage says that we face our responsibility to a larger society—friends, family, fellow Christians—as conscientiously as possible. We do not live to ourselves; we live as members of a community, whose approval is important, whose love is desired, whose reputation is esteemed.

Marriage under God and before an audience, marriage ratified by the laws of the state or province, is a strong statement of intention. It says we intend to worship God and depend on him; we intend to draw on and contribute to the welfare of our community; we intend to put our commitment now and our perseverance later on public record. Nothing less than this kind of statement will give our human relationships—especially our sexual relationships—the setting in which to thrive for our good and God's glory.

For further reading
H. Gollwitzer, *Song of Love*. Philadelphia: Fortress, 1978.
L. Smedes, *Sex for Christians*. Grand Rapids: Eerdmans, 1976.
V. M. Stewart, *Sexual Freedom*. Downers Grove, Ill.: IVP, 1974.
H. Thielicke, *The Ethics of Sex*. Grand Rapids: Baker, 1978.
W. Trobisch, *Living with Unfulfilled Desires*. Downers Grove, Ill.: IVP, 1979.
D. Tweedie, Jr., *The Christian and Sex*. Grand Rapids: Baker, 1964.
J. White, *Eros Defiled: The Christian and Sexual Sin*. Downers Grove, Ill.: IVP, 1977.

2

Homosexuality:

Why Can't I Love the Way I Want?

HER EYES WERE RIVETED TO my face as she carefully measured her words. I could tell from her body language—the tightness of her arms and the tension lines around her mouth—that something terribly painful was about to be said. I tried to support her in her anxieties by listening calmly and intently. Disinterest or impatience, shock or disapproval at that moment would have broken our communication. When the key sentence was finally extruded through clenched teeth, I knew why she had been wretched with anguish: "This weekend my mother told me that my daddy is a homosexual."

No response was appropriate but an encouraging sound or two and a gentle nod of the head that prompted her to let her feelings tumble out. Through hours of conversation over a number of months, I had learned much about her family. Its dynamics I had found strange. Now I began to comprehend more of the reasons: an unloved, rejected mother; a father forced to live with a dark secret; sisters without strong masculine influence to foster their femininity; a brother whose masculinity was so in jeopardy that he tried to find it by teasing his sisters almost to the point of torture.

All this in a Christian home that could have stood next to yours; all this in a Christian family that was faithful in church attendance and active in church service. That episode nearly twenty years ago was not my first acquaintance with the problems of homosexuals. But it certainly sharpened for me the pathos of the problem and alerted me to the effect it had on some of my own friends and neighbors.

Since that time the attention of almost every community has been directed to the presence of practicing homosexuals at every level of our society and in every vocation and profession. As a movement, homosexuals have become ever more vocal and, at times, militant.

"Why can't we love each other in the way we want?" is the question that they ask us. "Our style of loving," they press, "may be abnormal to you, but it is normal for us—not wrong, just different."

Their question and their claim put us Christians on the spot. We want to be as understanding as we can, yet all the while our biblical faith is raising yellow, if not red, flags in our minds. The problems are too huge, too varied, too complex, too painful, to submit to simple solutions. But we do need to search for guidelines that will help shape our attitudes and our actions as we face growing concerns about homosexuality.

The Need for Further Information
Homosexuality, perhaps more than any other of our social conditions, has been cloaked in mystery. Discussed only when children were not present—and then in whispers—it has been a subject on which most of us have been ignorant until recently. We have known that there are people with such tendencies, and we have either been glad that we did not share them or fearful lest we did.

But the causes of homosexual tendencies, the special inner problems that homosexuals face, the best ways to deal with such tendencies—all of these matters baffle most of us. Even professionals such as psychologists and psychiatrists disagree when these touchy subjects are raised.

One good result from the current fury in the news media is that our attention is called to a matter which deserves more light. *Research,* as thorough and scientific as possible, is badly needed. What aspects of homosexuality are innate and what are acquired? Are there genetic factors as well as psychic experiences that tilt people away from heterosexual relationships? What forms of psychotherapy seem to be most effective in changing the sexual outlook of a homosexual? What can a family do to head off homosexual tendencies once they are spotted? How can homosexuals learn to live responsibly with their urges? These and a host of other questions need to be brought out of the closet and dealt with as openly and effectively as are other issues in medical and psychological research.

Our Christian belief in God as Creator tells us that what we learn from human experience and scientific research has a validity worthy of our attention. Christian revelation is twofold: God speaks through his world and through his Word. The Bible, of course, is the final authority when it comes to Christian belief and Christian conduct, but a solid knowledge of the causes and effects of human behavior can be of substantial help in understanding and applying the teachings of Scripture to daily life. For example, medical research has now substantiated the concern that many Christians have had about the evils of smoking.

Theology as well as research must provide us further information. The key role of Christian theology in this matter is to remind us of the purpose of our sexuality. Why were we created male and female? Let us begin our answer with a look at Genesis.

So the LORD God caused a deep sleep to fall upon the man, and while he slept took one of his ribs and closed up its place with flesh; and the rib which the LORD God had taken from the man he made into a woman and brought her to the man. Then the man said,

"This at last is bone of my bones
   and flesh of my flesh;
she shall be called Woman,
   because she was taken out of Man."

Therefore a man leaves his father and his mother and cleaves to his wife, and they become one flesh.

And the man and his wife were both naked, and were not ashamed. (Gen. 2:21-25)

Unity and diversity—that is the theme of this passage. Man and woman are one in a way that man and animal can never be. Man and woman are different in a way that man and man or woman and woman cannot be.

It was this unity and diversity, a gift from the Creator's hand at creation, that formed the background of the biblical commands against intercourse with animals or intercourse with persons of the same sex: "You shall not lie with a male as with a woman; it is an abomination. And you shall not lie with any beast and defile yourself with it, neither shall any woman give herself to a beast to lie with it: it is perversion" (Lev. 18:22-23). Can we appreciate God's reason for these stern commands? He is condemning sexual experience that is not put to the purposes for which he intended it.

As we saw in chapter one, procreation, enjoyment and covenant were his high purposes when he made us male and female in his image. Procreation is impossible in a homosexual or bestial relationship. Though some enjoyment is undoubtedly possible, full enjoyment will not usually be possible because of the fear, anxiety, shame and guilt that may surround such relationships. And permanence of covenant is almost impossible outside of heterosexual marriage.

Fleeting liaisons, frantic but short-lived relationships tend to be the homosexual pattern. The stability of a good marriage with the balance brought by true masculinity and femininity is the only valid expression of the permanent covenant between God and his people, between Christ and his church.

This covenantal purpose of our sexuality, where we find true wholeness in a lasting bond with a partner of the opposite sex, is strengthened, not weakened, in the New Testament. Laws of diet and dress, of uncleanness and cleanness, the New Testament may set aside. Yet it is consistent with the Old Testament in its insistence that the genital expression of our human sexuality be confined to heterosexual relationships within the permanent covenant of marriage. Far from seeing homosexuality as an acceptable alternative, Paul saw it as the tragic result of our human rebellion in which we "exchanged the truth about God for a lie and worshiped and served the creature rather than the Creator, who is blessed for ever" (Rom. 1:25).

That foolish exchange led to dishonorable consequences: "Their women exchanged natural relations for unnatural, and the men likewise gave up natural relations with women and were consumed with passion for one another, men committing shameless acts with men and receiving in their own persons the due penalty for their error" (Rom. 1:26-27). In a dreadful spiral, idolatry led to perversion which, in turn, led to shame, guilt, disease and other forms of judgment.

Undoubtedly there is much more that Christian theologians and scholars need to learn about human sexuality and God's plan for it as revealed in the Bible. But we can know enough now to give no encouragement to society's trends to accept and condone homosexuality as a natural expression of our sexuality.

The Need for Stronger Discipline

What, then, should Christians do when they find themselves attracted to a homosexual relationship?

That question can shock us only if we are unaware of statistics. If it is true that one of ten persons in our society has some homosexual leanings, then literally millions of Christians are contending with the problem in some way. What should they do?

They should exercise Christian discipline, as all of us need to in the heat of temptation. They should stay away from relationships that increase the temptation. They should seek the fellowship of Christian individuals or groups who will help them live steady and stable lives.

Nothing in the Bible indicates that all Christians must marry. Celibate singleness is a perfectly acceptable Christian practice, as the lives of Jesus and Paul remind us. Persons attracted to members of the same sex should be encouraged to live fruitful and disciplined lives without sexual encounter. Where this proves uncontrollably difficult, professional help should be sought, preferably from a Christian psychologist.

There is a vast difference between homosexual tendencies and homosexual practices. One need not, by the grace of God, lead to the other.

The Need for Warmer Compassion

A word is needed to those of us who do not wrestle with homosexual tendencies. We, too, have a major need—the need for warmer compassion.

For too long we have tolerated cheap jokes about people who struggle with strong feelings. We have used stinging labels such as "fairy" or "queer" to demean them. Enough of that! The same Bible that bans homosexual unions encourages compassion for human suffering. Were it not for the grace of God, any of us could be caught in that same web.

Christian compassion seeks to love and help persons regardless of their plight. It knows that loving concern has much more healing power in it than harsh judgment.

Christian compassion remembers that all of us are given to vile practices which should have sent us to hell. Therefore, it refuses to label some sins as more heinous than others, and it places no sinners beyond the power of redemption.

Christian compassion recalls Paul's word about a whole list of sinners who stand outside the kingdom of God: "Do not be deceived; neither the immoral, nor idolaters, nor adulterers, nor sexual perverts, nor thieves, nor the greedy, nor drunkards, nor revilers, nor robbers will inherit the kingdom of God. And such were some of you. But you were washed, you were sanctified, you were justified in the name of the Lord Jesus Christ and in the Spirit of our God" (1 Cor. 6:9-11).

Above all, Christian compassion gives no snap answers and makes no easy judgments about matters as vexing as homosexuality. It seeks, rather, to live so that the cleansing changes and the daily power which we are experiencing as Christ's people will be shared with all who need them, including those precious persons whom God loves but who are confused about their sexual identity.

For further reading

E. Batchelor, Jr., ed., *Homosexuality and Ethics*. New York: Pilgrim, 1980.

J. Boswell, *Christianity, Social Tolerance, and Homosexuality*. Chicago: Univ. of Chicago Press, 1979.

A. Davidson, *The Returns of Love*. Downers Grove, Ill.: IVP, 1977.

D. Field, *The Homosexual Way–A Christian Option?* Downers Grove,

Ill.: IVP, 1979.
Nancy, *Homosexual Struggle*. Downers Grove, Ill.: IVP, 1980.
R. Lovelace, *Homosexuality and the Church*. Old Tappan, N.J.: Revell, 1978.
H. Thielicke, *The Ethics of Sex*. Grand Rapids: Baker, 1978.
D. Williams, *The Bond that Breaks: Will Homosexuality Split the Church?* Los Angeles: Bim, 1978.

3

Abortion:

It's My Body, Isn't It?

WE FACE AN ESPECIALLY sticky problem in our society. As Christians we are so surrounded by the values and attitudes of our fellow citizens that our conduct is strongly affected by theirs.

And this is not all bad. Ours is a reasonably civilized society, with growing sensitivity toward people disadvantaged because of race, income, occupation, sex and age. We have taken bounding steps in the last twenty years in our attempts to help the unfortunate. Often non-Christians have led the way in expressing concern for those whom earlier generations tended to neglect.

Yet on certain issues the consensus of our society raises large problems for us as Christians. Premarital sex is an example. As we have seen, the modern failure to grasp God's purposes for sex means that sex is treated as a matter of habit or appetite, a drive to be gratified, an instinct to be expressed. Divorce is another example, for easy attitudes toward marriage have allowed people to dissolve partnerships as readily as they change apartments or transfer from one job to another. I now dread reunions with people I have not seen recently. The talk inevitably turns to which of our acquaintances are no longer living together. Convenience and compatibility have overwhelmed the covenant as a basis for marriage.

It is hard to swim against these tides. The literature we read, the dramas we watch, the conversations we hear, the opinions which learned people express—these all blow winds contrary to the values and ideals we treasure. In seas like these, it is easy to lose confidence and wonder who is right—they or we?

Huge sectors of our society claim abortion on demand as the right of any pregnant woman. Particularly vocal have been some advocates of women's rights. Pregnancy is a peculiarly feminine problem, they have argued. Only the woman in question can properly decide whether or not to carry the baby to term. "It's my body, isn't it?" has become their rallying cry.

Their predicament sparks sympathy within the toughest of us. Bearing an unwanted child is surely no picnic. The long, weary months of pregnancy bring anxiety and fatigue even to eager mothers. What must be the emotions of those for whom childbirth will mean embarrassment, shame, financial burden, changed plans, reordered priorities?

There will be sympathy for all who face unwanted pregnancy. But along with sympathy will go understanding and conviction if our response is to be truly Christian. Our attitude toward abortion will not be determined primarily by what our society believes or even what the Supreme Court of our nation decides. Biblical insights about life and its meaning will outrank even the consensus of all the wise and admirable people around us.

True, the problem is sticky, but we must let its difficulty make us more diligent to hear the will of God. Hearing God's will in the matter of abortion is not simple; indeed, there is no single Scripture verse, no one passage, that can set the matter straight. We must try to discover the counsel of God by weighing teachings from many parts of Scripture.

We are focusing on abortion on demand. The more complex matter of therapeutic abortion is beyond our reach here. We are not concentrating on the few exceptions so often raised in discussion: babies conceived in incest or rape, or mothers whose lives may be endangered through childbirth. Today they are a handful in comparison with the hundreds of thousands of women who seek relief from pregnancies that they find inconvenient. As Christians, we will want to keep certain biblical principles in mind.

A Concern for Life

None of us should take life for granted. A sturdy redwood tree that presides over the garden behind our apartment continually reminds me of that. For nearly three years I watched with distress as its foliage turned brittle and brown. Recently new neighbors assumed its care. They tore out the brick patio that had choked life from its trunk and began to water it as liberally as our semidrought conditions in California allow. I gaze at it now as I write these words.

Green new life is crowding out the brown up and down its seventy-five feet of trunk and branches. The Creator's hand is again at work, as surely as it was on that third day when God called redwoods and other green growth into being with these words: " 'Let the earth put forth vegetation, plants yielding seed, and fruit trees bearing fruit in which is their seed, each according to its kind, upon the earth' " (Gen. 1:11). It was this creative event that Joyce Kilmer had in mind when he wrote, "Poems, [he might have said "sermons"] are made by fools like me, but only God can make a tree."

If a redwood alive from the dead delights us with the power and mystery of our Creator, what should the wonder of human conception do? Coded into a tiny egg and microscopic sperm, God has placed all the potential for personhood. From that obscure beginning comes the fullness of human life, surely one of his greatest gifts.

In a way that not even a giant and ancient redwood can boast, the fusion of mother's egg and father's sperm bears the image of God. The capacity to subdue the earth by skill and technology, the gift of human relationships in love and care, the capability of communion with the living God—these high gifts are packaged in a conception no larger than the dot that tops an *i* on this page.

A human fetus is tiny, helpless, powerless and nameless as it clings for life to the wall of a mother's womb. But it is also a powerful statement from God about human life and destiny, about human fellowship with God now and in the world to come. No Christian can treat conception as a mere biological accident. Behind all life stands the loving and mighty Creator, especially behind human life which uniquely bears his image. Our Christian concern for life makes us hate war, loathe murder, suspect euthanasia and question genetic meddling. That same concern for life can never allow us to make abortion a casual affair.

A Commitment to Justice

The Bible champions the cause of the underdog. David's defeat of Goliath and Israel's victory over the pharaoh are more than episodes of biblical history, though they certainly were historical events. They are pictures of the difference between the way God views life and the way we usually view it. The influential, the powerful, the rich, the mighty—these are the people we cheer and want to emulate. In the decades when the New York Yankees dominated baseball with the likes of Lou Gehrig, Joe Dimaggio and Mickey Mantle, I was an avid Yankee fan. When they slumped into obscurity in the late 1960s, my interest slumped as well. Now that they have returned to prominence I find my own enthusiasm pumped up again.

I am not much like God. His commitment is frequently to people who seem to be losers—widows, orphans, oppressed people, strangers in the land who have little wealth and less protection. Champions come and go, but God is constant in his concern for the underprivileged:

Father of the fatherless and protector of widows

is God in his holy habitation. (Ps. 68:5)

Furthermore, he judges how righteous we are as his people on the basis of our commitment to justice:

> Wash yourselves; make yourselves clean;
> > remove the evil of your doings
> > from before my eyes;
> cease to do evil, learn to do good;
> > seek justice, correct oppression;
> defend the fatherless, plead for the widow. (Is. 1:16-17)

Active justice that seeks to undo wrongs, compassionate justice that guards the rights of the powerless, effective justice that knows how easy it is to abuse those who have no defender—that is God's view of justice. It must become ours.

Only one biblical passage deals with the death of an unborn child. It discusses compensation in the case of a woman who miscarries because of some act of violence done to her. If she herself is not harmed, "the one who hurt her shall be fined, according as the woman's husband shall lay upon him; and he shall pay as the judges determine. If any harm follows [to the woman], then you shall give life for life, eye for eye, tooth for tooth" (Ex. 21:22-24). This interpretation of the passage is supported by virtually all modern translations. It is worth noting, however, that the Hebrew text itself is more ambiguous as to who is harmed in the accident, the mother alone or the mother and the child. It is possible that the miscarriage (v. 22) may describe a premature live birth, in which case there is no harm, or the delivery of a stillborn baby, in which case there is harm and therefore, according to verse 23, death would be the appropriate punishment. This interpretation would make the strongest possible case against abortion—virtually equating it with murder. Lack of specificity in the text itself leads me to shy away from this equation.

The people of biblical times so valued conception and childbirth as a blessing of God, an economic security and a way of carrying on the father's name that self-inflicted abortion would have been very uncommon. When abortion was caused by someone else, as described in the passage above, a fine was exacted as compensation for the destroyed fetus and the subsequent loss to the parents. It is hard to extract a great deal of meaning for us from this episode, but it is certainly safe to say that miscarriage was of sufficient seriousness in the will of God to call for a specific and detailed law to deal with it.

The biblical commitment to justice, as I see it, can be extended to the matter of abortion. If God has a concern for the defenseless and asks us to share that concern, then that concern should also be extended to the unborn baby. Is not abortion on demand a form of injustice or oppression? A fetus can make no speeches in court, carry no placards in front of the state house, hire no lawyer to plead its cause. "It's my body," a perplexed mother may say, "and I have my rights." But do not biblical people always ask about the rights of others? And are we not especially concerned for those who are unable to stand up for their rights?

A Caution about the Drastic

As Christians, we are different. We are concerned for life that God has made in his image; we are committed to justice for the helpless whom God loves; and we are cautious about taking any drastic action, especially drastic action that we cannot repair.

We do not support torture as punishment, for instance. We know how selfishly sinful we can be. We know how capable our fallen humanity is of harshness, rashness, cruelty. We approve laws that protect us and others from such acts. Because abortion is so drastic, so final, we should treat the subject with extreme caution.

We must also be cautious because we know how guilty we can feel about an act done in haste, particularly when that act is irreparable. Abortion is far too complex to be a medical decision alone. The psychic and spiritual damage that it can do may be weighty beyond words.

The Supreme Court of the United States has left the decision of abortion to the mother and her physician. Christians will want more than medical help.

The preciousness of sex as a covenant relationship, the mystery of conception as a gift of the Creator, the concern for the rights of the fetus, the knowledge of the drastic nature of abortion—all of these should prompt God's people to develop attitudes toward pregnancy that our contemporary society may not understand.

Christians are under higher orders. As we take these orders seriously we see that our rights can give way to God's will. And when we do, we can count on his help not only to be different from the world but to rejoice in that difference.

For further reading
N. Anderson, *Issues of Life and Death*. Downers Grove, Ill.: IVP, 1976.
C. Bajema, *Abortion and the Meaning of Persons*. Grand Rapids: Baker, 1974.

R. Gardner, *Abortion: The Personal Drama*. Grand Rapids: Eerdmans, 1972.

J. Mohr, *Abortion in America*. New York: Oxford Univ. Press, 1978.

P. Ramsey, *Ethics at the Edge of Life; Medical and Legal Intersections*. New Haven: Yale Univ. Press, 1978.

F. Schaeffer and C. E. Koop, *Whatever Happened to the Human Race?* Old Tappan, N.J.: Revell, 1979.

J. Shelly, *Dilemma: A Nurse's Guide for Making Ethical Decisions*. Downers Grove, Ill.: IVP, 1980.

H. Thielicke, *The Ethics of Sex*. Grand Rapids: Baker, 1978.

4

Pornography:

It Won't Harm Me, Will It?

TODAY, PORNOGRAPHY IS almost inescapable. What used to be slipped from under the counter in a plain brown wrapper now shouts its obscenities from the sales stands in drugstores and supermarkets. What once was circulated with a smirk at a stag party is now available to young and old for fifty cents from an automatic vending machine. Sexually explicit scenes that would have been censored by the "Hayes Office" in my childhood are now nightly fare on prime-time television. Plots that would have been banned in Boston during the forties are portrayed openly in a dozen daily soap operas. "Peyton Place," with all its scandal a few decades ago, seems almost as calm as "Sesame Street" to today's audiences.

The availability and intensity of pornography call us as Christians to take a good look at our standards and values. Apparently even the better resources in our land will not help us much. Our courts, for instance, have had great difficulty articulating guidelines to curtail the circulation of lurid materials without censoring materials that have a legitimate medical or artistic purpose. Enforcing the guidelines has proved even harder than developing them. Very few X-rated movies, books or magazines have been permanently withdrawn from circulation by judicial verdicts.

Many city and town councils are puzzled as to how to restrict the invasion of bookstores, movie houses and massage parlors that pander to the pornographic tastes of our society. As Christians we can support the efforts of wise judges, responsible legislators and concerned council members, but we must do much more.

In the long run, pornography's harm will not depend on court decisions or legislative action. The degree of its damage will directly relate to our understanding of why pornography is dangerous and how Christians should view sexuality.

As in the other sexual matters—premarital sex, homosexuality, abortion—we cannot take our standards from the prevailing attitudes of the world. We cannot sew the silk purse of Christian responsibility from the sow's ear of secular values. Against the luridness of the slick centerfold we must pit the steadiness of the Hebrew-Christian Scriptures. They are our guide in all matters of godly belief and practice.

The Creator's Purposes

For biblical people, back to basics always means back to the Garden of Eden. The words that catch our eye for this subject are these: "And the man and his wife were both naked, and were not ashamed" (Gen. 2:25). Here we are reminded that nakedness itself was our state from the beginning. (Not that we need that reminder, since each of us has been born in that same state.) We picked up clothes along the way; we did not bring them with us into the world.

The nakedness of Adam and Eve at the beginning was delightful for two reasons: (1) their nakedness was evidence of the beauty present in all creation, every part of which, especially our human face and form, God called good and (2) their nakedness was a symbol of their capacity for intimate relationship in the covenant of marriage. They admired each other's bodies, and they longed to be one flesh.

All of this went awry in the next scene. When they became rivals of God, rather than his servants, the man and the woman yielded to the serpent's suggestion and ate the outlawed fruit: "Then the eyes of both were opened, and they knew that they were naked; and they sewed fig leaves together and made themselves aprons" (Gen. 3:7). Glory in their beauty turned to shame of their nakedness when they rebelled against the Creator—a shame so deep that the man and his wife hid from their Lord: "And he [the man] said, 'I heard the sound of thee in the garden, and I was afraid, because I was naked; and I hid myself.' [God] said, 'Who told you that you were naked? Have you eaten of the tree of which I commanded you not to eat?' " (Gen. 3:10-11). Yet even the attempt of the man and woman to clothe their nakedness was to no avail, so that they needed God to come to their rescue: "And the LORD God made for Adam and for his wife garments of skins, and clothed them" (3:21).

The story in brief: nakedness with no shame; nakedness with great shame. In between, we read about the great disobedience and the futile efforts at self-correction through trying to hide and stitching fig leaves.

How does this story relate to the problem of pornography? It reminds us that nudity was part of the Creator's purpose from the beginning. It is attractive; it is touched with the beauty of the master Artist's handiwork.

But it also reminds us that nudity, this side of the Fall, is hard for us to deal with. Admiration readily turns to lust; openness can lead to shame. The basic problem is not nudity, for God made us that way. Rather, it is our perverse response to it. That is our fault, the result of our failure to maintain proper relationships with God and each other. We were made male and female in his image, but we have wrongly used our sexuality. Either we give vent to it in lust and become promiscuous or we resist it in shame and become prudish or even frigid.

God's answer was to provide cover for us. In other words, random nakedness is not in our best interest. It is too hot for us to handle. Whether in print, on stage or in pictures, it prompts responses that are out of harmony with the Creator's purposes—admiration of the beauty of his work or enjoyment of the intimacy of the marriage covenant.

The Proper Context

The Song of Solomon gives us a picture of a true expression of sexual attraction. It reminds us that the Bible is not against sex, only against the improper use of it. This "best of songs" (as the book's alternate title, Song of Songs, can be translated) speaks to the problem of pornography by putting sex in its proper context. Pornography typically has two great shortcomings: (1) it centers in the physical organs and techniques of sex and (2) it seeks increased excitement by changing partners or even using multiple partners. In short, pornography suffers from being partial and fickle. In contrast, consider the beautiful picture of sexual attraction in the Song of Solomon.

Sex is enjoyed in the context of full appreciation for the other person. Of course, the body of the partner is appreciated. The bride's dovelike eyes, graceful hair, perfect teeth, scarlet lips, erect neck and charming breasts all are praised by her lover (4:1-5). At the same time the husband's locks, eyes, cheeks, lips, arms, body and legs are singled out for admiration by his woman (5:10-15).

But the relationship is more than bodily:

His speech is most sweet,
 and he is altogether desirable. (5:16)

Conversation and fellowship are as important as physical intimacy. Indeed, the tone of the entire Song is rich with the regard and esteem that the two have for each other. It is the whole person, not just the body, that has captured the interest of each.

The pornographic camera does not do that. It zooms in on the body or bodies and fixes on the physical features. The emotions, the spiritual qualities, the personal needs of the people involved are all overlooked. Sex becomes a mechanical exercise, not a total expression of affection for the other person. The Song of Solomon knows better.

Sex is enjoyed in the context of total commitment to the other person:

> Set me as a seal upon your heart,
> as a seal upon your arm;
> for love is strong as death,
> jealousy is cruel as the grave....
> Many waters cannot quench love,
> neither can floods drown it.
> If a man offered for love
> all the wealth of his house,
> it would be utterly scorned. (8:6-7)

An exclusive relationship—each partner sealed to the other in the covenant of marriage—that is the context in which sexual attraction and sexual expression are to be experienced.

In contrast, pornographic novels and films trace the adventures of their heroes and heroines through a series of affairs or even orgies. The passion, then, is only physical and transient. The pilgrimage of such people resembles that of the gourmet who takes delight in visiting restaurants and rating their menus. Such promiscuity has nothing to do with a love which "is strong as death."

The Concern for Love

All Christian conduct needs to pass the test of love. Preoccupation with pornography fails this test at several points.

Pornography neglects love for others. Those who earn their living by it are exploited financially and treated as less than human, as sex objects, by those who produce the pornographic works. To support pornography is to contribute to the hurt of the people involved. The use of children in pornographic enterprises is such an unspeakable breach of love that it needs no comment.

Neighborhoods suffer where pornographic activities flourish. Residents are degraded; crime may increase; the underworld may be attracted. To allow this, and especially to contribute to it, is unloving.

Marriage partners are often badly hurt by pornography. Few men and women can rival the figures of centerfold models. Use of pornography can make one partner dissatisfied with the other.

Finally, the use of pornography can hurt the love we should have for ourselves. It can lead to guilt that makes us edgy and quarrelsome. It can lead to fantasies about sex that fill our minds with lust. It can lead to concentration on the physical that makes us less sensitive to our emotional and spiritual needs. In short it may seduce us to a view of sexuality which robs us of the full joy that God intends.

We are all potential pornographers. Our imaginations can conjure up scenes with great dexterity. The works of the flesh, this side of Eden, are realities with which we all must reckon. Among them Paul listed "Fornication, impurity, licentiousness." There is nothing casual about them: "I warn you, as I warned you before, that those who do such things shall not inherit the kingdom of God" (Gal. 5:19, 21). We need forgiveness even as we try to resist temptation.

The best defense against those sexual works of the flesh is a loving, stable marriage. Where the biblical purposes of admiring beauty and experiencing the covenant are a daily reality, the Spirit of God will be at work to grow his fruit of "love, joy, peace, patience ... self-control" (Gal. 5:22-23). Where open, warm, abiding love is the rule, partners will be loyal, children will be secure, and temptations will be warded off.

Not that the fruit of the Spirit can be cultivated only in the garden of matrimony. Singles too have resources available to support their desires for purity. With all Christians, they can know a freedom that springs from forgiveness, a freedom that releases us from both nagging guilt about our X-rated thoughts and compulsive fascination with them, a freedom that focuses on "the things that are above" (Col. 3:1-5). Likewise they have God's exhortation to think about the honorable, the just, the pure, the lovely, the praiseworthy (Phil. 4:8). Even more they have the Bible's help in defining those precious qualities, especially as they were displayed in Jesus' life.

Pornography is almost inescapable. But its damage can be curtailed. In all our endeavors to lead righteous lives, our holy Father stands ready to answer the petitions which we learned from his Son: "And lead us not into temptation, But deliver us from evil" (Mt. 6:13).

For further reading

J. Court, *Pornography: A Christian Critique*. Downers Grove, Ill.: IVP, 1980.

C. Curran, *Issues in Sexual and Medical Ethics*. South Bend, Ind.: Notre Dame Press, 1980.

G. Parrinder, *Sex in the World's Religions*. New York: Oxford Univ. Press, 1980.

H. Thielicke, *The Ethics of Sex*. Grand Rapids: Baker, 1978.

5

Women's Rights:

Why Can't I Be Treated As a Person?

ALL DAY THE TIME-CHECKS ON our local radio station had the same ring: KFWB equal time 10:15; KFWB equal time 12:17; equal time, equal time. Like the persistent tolling of a bell, the announcers, usually women that day, chimed home the reminder that women's rights need our full attention. The day was August 26, the fifty-seventh anniversary of the constitutional amendment giving women the right to vote.

Equal time is a worthy emphasis for our generation. We are part of a culture that has not always treated women fairly. Ours is a tainted history: we have limited the roles that women can take; we have denied them full rights to education, employment and equal compensation; we have assumed that they have little aptitude for financial matters, business administration or technical vocations; we have viewed them as emotional in their decision making and unreliable as credit risks. No wonder the women of our society are crying out in a mounting crescendo, "Why can't I be treated as a person?"

Ours is, in many ways, a man's world. It has been increasingly painful for me to recognize prejudices that I need to overcome, if I am to respond to the call of women who have felt put down, misused, even oppressed.

My pain has been aggravated by the fact that throughout Christian history, the Bible has been wrongly and cruelly used as a rod to beat women into submission. Just as well-meaning people misapplied the Scriptures to justify slavery, some have cramped women into second-class berths on the basis of a ticket that the Bible supposedly furnished.

Equal time—women in our day deserve it. So does the Bible, for it has suffered much at the hands of many. What does it actually say about women's rights? When adequately understood, it becomes a bill of women's rights, an emancipation proclamation to the misused and misled everywhere.

The Right to Full Fellowship with God

No biblical discussion of personhood can make any progress unless it begins with the Genesis account of our creation. Like an anchor, that story keeps us from drifting onto the shoals of relativity where so many ships have foundered in our time. If our personhood were merely part of a mindless, chancy evolutionary process, then biology would become our guide to life. The struggle for equality among the sexes would be only part of a genetic game, a way of securing the survival of feminine genes. The current battle for personhood would be just a phase in the evolutionary warfare which finds nature bloody in tooth and claw.

Yet even those who do not take their cues from the Bible seem to recognize that more is involved in dealing with sexual prejudice than an episode in the history of adaptation. The quest for full acceptance as persons is of greater significance than the development of fatty layers to protect the organs of cold-water mammals or the development of variegated skin colors to match the foliage where the chameleon may hide.

Most people hold human personhood to be unique, even if they do not know why. Biblical people know that our personhood is the result of God's creation and sets us apart from the rest of creation. We may share certain skeletal features and biological processes. But there is something about us that biology alone can not explain. It is that something—that mystery of personality—that is at stake in the insistence of women that they be treated as persons.

Then God said, "Let us make man in our image, after our likeness; and let them have dominion over the fish of the sea, and over the birds of the air, and over the cattle, and over all the earth, and over every creeping thing that creeps upon the earth." So God created man in his own image, in the image of God he created him; male and female he created them. And God blessed them, and God said to them, "Be fruitful and multiply, and fill the earth and subdue it; and have dominion over the fish of the sea and over the birds of the air and over every living thing that moves upon the earth." (Gen. 1:26-28)

Note the pointers to human uniqueness in those words: (1) the formula of creation has changed from "let there be" to "let us make," as though God were giving more personal attention to the work of the sixth day; (2) the human family—male and female—is to have dominion over the rest of creation; (3) human maleness and femaleness—the capacity for fellowship—is part of what God means by creation in his image; and (4) God specifically blessed the man and the woman (the Bible's first mention of blessing) as a father would bless his children. Note that the woman is fully included in the process because she is created in God's image, she shares in the dominion and she receives the blessing. She has full rights of personhood.

At the heart of these rights is the right to full fellowship with God. How are we made in God's image? How are we like him? Do we look like him? I think not; God does not share our limitations of bone and blood. Are we divine as he is divine? Of course not. Our wisdom, power, love, and holiness are all limited; his are not.

How are we like him? In personhood. In the capacity to know, to feel, to remember, to love, to call each other by name, to say "you" to the other person—in this remarkable capacity, in this unique ability we are like God. We can talk to him, and we can understand what he says to us. To pray and to worship, these are distinctively human acts. Full right to personhood means, at heart, full right to know and love

God. Men and women—God's special creatures—share that capacity and that opportunity.

But this fellowship with God, based on creation, must be guided by Scripture. In Genesis 3 we discover that equally and together, the man and the woman violated God's command. Rebellion replaced their fellowship with God; competition displaced their fellowship with each other.

Equal time, the radio station hammered every few minutes. The hammering was necessary because we as fallen men have shown our selfishness in wanting to train women to suit our purposes whether it was best for them or not.

Yet the call of equal time today will not be enough. Biblical insights are needed to keep equal time from becoming another form of selfishness—a female form. When the women's movement wants the right to demand abortion at will, it needs to listen to God's Word about the sanctity of life that God has created. When the women's movement (including some within the church) wants lesbianism to be accepted as normal, it needs to listen to God's Word about the purposes of sexuality as the basis of a permanent covenant between a man and a woman. When the women's movement turns hostile and bitter toward masculinity, it needs to hear the Word of God about love for neighbor and compassion toward an enemy.

The Bible offers all men and women the right to full fellowship with God. Without that fellowship, guided by the teachings of Scripture, there can be no true personhood.

The Right to Full Partnership in Christ

To the Galatians Paul uttered one of history's grand

proclamations—the announcement that distinction of race, sex and station had nothing to do with God's approval: "There is neither Jew nor Greek, there is neither slave nor free, there is neither male nor female; for you are all one in Christ Jesus. And if you are Christ's, then you are Abraham's offspring, heirs according to promise" (3:28-29). This means nothing less than women's right to total partnership in Christ's redemptive plan. In God's book only one thing counts: wholehearted loyalty to him because of what Jesus has done for us. Erased are all the distinctions that people make about one race, one sex or one economic state being higher or better than another. Believers are one in Christ and, therefore, in Abraham, the father of all the faithful. In other words, all who truly trust Christ are full partners who will share the riches that God promised Abraham and his kin.

Why can't you as a woman be treated as a person? The gospel's answer is plain: you *have* been, in the love Jesus showed to you and the work he has done for you. The grace of forgiveness released from his cross, the power for new life triggered by his resurrection, the victory over fear and superstition sparked by his ascension, the prayer for our welfare raised in his present relationship with God—all of these know no gender. They are for female and male alike. Nothing offers equal time like the gospel.

If the freedom of the gospel means that the distinctions between men and women in spiritual privileges are no longer binding, what are the down-to-earth results? (1) The new life brought by the gospel is the life that God wants us all to lead. (2) In that life, false interpretations of female or male dominance are done away with. (3) Therefore, we as Christians, sons and daughters of Christ and Abraham, should seek to demonstrate that new life. (4) We should treat all people with the dignity and worth that the gospel grants them and do our best to put down prejudice and bigotry wherever they exist, starting, perhaps, in our own homes.

The gospel promises all women and men the right to full partnership in Christ. Without that partnership, true personhood will be a fantasy unrealized.

The Right to Full Ministry in the Holy Spirit
God is the Creator, the source of our right to fellowship. Jesus is the Savior, the provider of our right to partnership. The Holy Spirit is the giver of gifts, the sponsor of our right to ministry.

All who trust Christ as Savior become partners in his church, made one by the Holy Spirit who indwells each person and binds us to God and to one another in his family. Each person in that church is a minister. Christ's ministry is carried on not primarily by a cadre of specially appointed individuals but by the whole church, the entire body. To every member of the body some spiritual gift has been given. (Lists of them are found in Romans 12, 1 Corinthians 12, Ephesians 4 and 1 Peter 4.) Nowhere is any distinction made between men and women in the receiving of these gifts.

Christian churches need to spend much more time evaluating the spiritual gifts that each member has been given, especially the women. We are often unspiritual in our selection of church leadership. We thrust people into office on the basis of income, prestige, loyalty, regard for feelings and a host of other bad reasons. We must obey the Spirit. When he gives gifts of evangelism or administration or prophecy or hospitality to his men and women, he expects the church to honor those gifts and to follow the leadership of those who have them.

Spiritual gifts convey to all Christ's men and women the right to full ministry. Without that ministry, personhood is restricted to less than what God desires.

Equal time, equal time—the radio announcer's cadence should be a reminder to us as men and an encouragement to us as women. God's people—made in his image, freed by his gospel, gifted by his Spirit—should point the way to a new life, where full personhood is enjoyed by those who belong to Christ and offered to those who do not, female and male alike.

For further reading
W. Chafe, *Women and Equality*. New York: Oxford Univ. Press, 1977.
P. Gundry, *Heirs Together*. Grand Rapids: Zondervan, 1978.
P. Jewett, *Man as Male and Female*. Grand Rapids: Eerdmans, 1975.
D. Williams, *The Apostle Paul and Women in the Church*. Glendale, Cal.: Regal, 1979.

6

Capital Punishment:

Isn't Killing Always Wrong?

SCARCELY ANY ISSUE WILL start a debate more quickly than this one. Take the prolonged dispute in California, for instance. A few years ago, a state-wide election indicated that California's citizens overwhelmingly supported the use of capital punishment in the case of certain more flagrant murders, especially where law enforcement officers or prison guards are the victims. Our state legislators, in both our assembly and senate, then responded to this public sentiment by passing laws to allow capital punishment under carefully prescribed circumstances. The governor of California, on the other hand, opposed the legislators, even though the vast majority of them were members of his own party, by vetoing their bill. The legislature then summoned the necessary two-thirds majority to override the veto and make the bill law. The controversy is not at all settled, because both the California and the United States Supreme Courts may well declare the entire bill or parts of it unconstitutional when test cases are brought before them.

California's conflict in this matter is only a small sample of the debate's intensity. The issues are substantial: on the one hand, human life, often that of one from an oppressed and disadvantaged background; and, on the other, society's protection, particularly of those whose precarious task is to enforce our laws.

Extremists on both sides are not hard to find. Some are willing to use almost any kind of force or violence to destroy a vicious criminal. In the past they exercised their convictions by joining lynch mobs and enforcing justice with a strong rope and a stout tree. Others view any taking of life as flagrant murder, whether by the state or by the individual. Frequently they blame society for all personal crimes committed, turning culprits into "helpless victims" and assuming that the basic purpose of a penal system is to rehabilitate people whom society has led astray.

Neither of those extremes has taken its cues from the Bible, certainly not from hearing the Bible's whole message on the matter. At heart, the approach to capital punishment that anyone takes will be related to that person's understanding of the nature and purpose of law. The teachings of both testaments can help

The Old Testament Establishes Our Regard for Law

Since we derive our humanity from him, God has never been reluctant to prescribe rules for our conduct and to determine the punishment should those rules be broken. What is his first word to Adam, if not an announcement of law and punishment?" You may freely eat of every tree of the garden; but of the tree of the knowledge of good and evil you shall not eat, for in the day that you eat of it you shall die" (Gen. 2:16-17). In a sense, capital punishment, or the possibility of it, began even before the Fall.

The flood in Noah's time cut the cords of history, except for a few strands. When the waters receded and life began again, Noah and his family received blessings and instructions from God quite like those to the first man and woman: "Be fruitful and multiply, and fill the earth. The fear of you and the dread of you shall be upon every beast of the earth... bird of the air... and all the fish of the sea" (Gen. 9:1-2). The command to multiply and the promise of dominion are the same as at the beginning (1:28), as is the provision of food (9:3; 1:29).

There is also a prohibition—not the eating of a certain fruit but the consuming of meat with the blood yet in it (9:4). Then immediately God added something new: "For your lifeblood I will surely require a reckoning; of every beast I will require it and of man; of every man's brother I will require the life of man. Whoever sheds the blood of man, by man shall his blood be shed; for God made man in his own image" (9:5-6).

Murder had badly marred history's first start as

Cain slew Abel (chap. 4); murder was not to be tolerated at history's second start, or any time thereafter. Regard for God's law, especially for those laws that guard human life, was established in the Old Testament. Nothing that has happened since should dampen that regard.

But doesn't capital punishment violate the basic command against killing found in the Ten Commandments (Ex. 20:13)? The biblical authors found no contradiction here, nor did the men of Israel whose task it was to enforce the laws. Why not? Because they knew that the commandment referred to murder, the lawless taking of life. The word used in the Hebrew text almost always is used in contexts involving premeditated murder or reckless manslaughter. The true meaning of the commandment is brought out in the New American Standard Bible ("You shall not murder") and in the New English Bible ("You shall not commit murder"). When the elders of Israel carried out the command given to Noah and the laws given to Moses, taking the life of a proven murderer, they were themselves free from all guilt.

What were the purposes of capital punishment? The first and foremost is that stated in the command to Noah: "Whoever sheds the blood of man, by man shall his blood be shed; for God made man in his own image" (Gen. 9:6). The sanctity of human life, the only life made in God's image, is the chief reason why capital punishment was instituted. It became the role of government, as the agency established to protect human rights, to insure that the unique value of human life was held in esteem. It is worth noting that the stress on God's image in the human family comes after the tragic Fall and after the disastrous flood. As rebellious as human life had become, as sinful as human personality had demonstrated itself to be, it still bore (though in a depraved and perverse way) the marks of God's personhood.

A second purpose of capital punishment was the dignity and welfare of society. To have integrity a society must take its standards seriously. Its dignity is compromised when it does not insist that those who break the law pay the price. As a doting parent who threatens but does not follow through loses the respect of a youngster, so a society that does not act on the laws that protect its citizens is disdained by its members, especially those who hold law in low regard. Corruption, degradation and lawlessness often follow.

Beyond that, a society needs to protect itself from the contaminating influence of lawlessness, which can spread like cancer and infect others. Our human bent toward sinning needs little example or encouragement. We are slanted in the direction of wrongdoing this side of Adam's fall, and we need the help of strong laws and solid enforcement to protect ourselves and others from the ingrained and explosive character of sin. A rebellious son was such a threat to clan life that he could not be tolerated in ancient Israel. He had to be dealt with to deter complete social upheaval: "Then all the men of the city shall stone him to death with stones; so you shall purge the evil from your midst; and all Israel shall hear, and fear" (Deut. 21:21).

Finally, strong punishment, including capital punishment, may be necessary for the survival of a given society. We recognize that, almost instinctively, in times of emergency. People throughout the

United States were incensed when they saw pictures of the burning and looting of New York shops and business firms during a summer power failure. At such times, as in the Santa Barbara fire where two hundred homes were burned or in the Johnstown flood where whole areas of the town had to be abandoned, crisis measures are necessary. Even the taking of life by peace officers or national guardsmen may be justified for the stability of the society and the general welfare of its citizens. Anarchy—wild violations of the personal and property rights of others—cannot be tolerated. It will destroy the decent processes by which we govern ourselves, and it will open the door to the indecent processes of totalitarian and oppressive government.

The New Testament Deepens Our Regard for Law

The principles of law and punishment laid down by God and his people in the Old Testament are deepened and strengthened in the New Testament. They were deepened by Jesus when he taught us to look to the spirit as well as the letter of the law. Not only murder but also hatred is a capital offense in God's eyes. Not only the adulterous act but also the lustful look merits stoning. Jesus helped us see what lawbreakers we all are, and how much taming by God's grace and God's Spirit it takes for us to live decent and responsible lives.

The principles of law and punishment were strengthened by Paul when he helped his friends at Rome understand that citizenship in God's kingdom meant respect, not disdain, for human government: "For rulers are not a terror to good conduct, but to bad. Would you have no fear of him who is in authority? Then do what is good, and you will receive his approval, for he is God's servant for your good. But if you do wrong, be afraid, for he does not bear the sword in vain; he is the servant of God to execute his wrath on the wrongdoer" (Rom. 13:3-4). The mention of the sword and the execution of God's wrath admits at least the possibility of capital punishment.

Both Testaments Insist on Just Process for Punishment

To biblical people *how* we do something is as important as *what* we do. The process can not be separated from the results. We cannot call for the possibility of capital punishment without a concern for the procedures.

Further, we cannot apply the biblical pattern without adapting it to current circumstances. Idolatry and sorcery, for instance, were both capital crimes in the book of Exodus (22:18, 20). Would any of us lobby for similar laws to be enforced today? Stoning and burning were the usual forms of execution in the Bible. Would they be acceptable in Toronto or San Francisco? If, therefore, we are to hold to the possibility of capital punishment as a means of reverencing life, we must do so on the basis of biblical principle, not on the basis of a literal application of biblical laws. And we must insist that other biblical values like the following also be respected.

Careful evaluation of the circumstances of a crime is utterly essential. Biblical law clearly distinguished self-defense from murder: "If a thief is found breaking in, and is struck so that he dies, there shall be no bloodguilt for him" (Ex. 22:2). It also distinguished accidental killing from premeditated: "If any one kills his neighbor unintentionally without having been at enmity with him in time past [the example given is an accident while chopping wood] . . . he may flee to one of these cities [of refuge] and save his life" (Deut. 19:4-5).

Every step must be taken to assure a fair trial. Good judges are indispensable: "You shall appoint judges and officers in all your towns . . . and they shall judge the people with righteous judgment. You shall not pervert justice; you shall not show partiality; and you shall not take a bribe" (Deut. 16:18-19). Honest witnesses are the backbone of the judicial processes: "You shall not bear false witness against your neighbor" (Ex. 20:16); "a single witness shall not prevail against a man for any crime . . . ; only on the evidence of two witnesses, or of three witnesses, shall a charge be sustained" (Deut. 19:15). Full protection of the rights of the accused must be guaranteed. That was the purpose of the cities of refuge to which one who had accidentally killed someone could flee until proper investigation could take place.

The whole community must take responsibility for capital punishment if it is employed. Old Testament law called for the witnesses to cast the first stones—a good way of testing the truthfulness of the witnesses—then the whole community joined in. Justice, in all its forms, is not solely the responsibility of judges, lawyers and police. It is a prime duty of all of us as citizens to promote it in every way. Christians know how important justice is to the heart of God and to the good of all people. Christians know how readily our human sinfulness subverts the cause of justice. We must lead the way.

In the dilemma between hard-line and soft-line

treatment of capital criminals, Christians must vocally and ardently and persistently call for a fair line. The Bible's support of capital punishment gives us no right to allow judicial short cuts. If we press for strong laws we must press equally for evenhanded justice. The Lord who loves rich and poor, black and white, male and female, the God who reads all hearts and speaks all languages without an accent, insists that we do this. He is the ultimate judge, and to him any failure to work for full justice for every man and woman would indeed be a capital crime.

For further reading
N. Anderson, *Issues of Life and Death*. Downers Grove, Ill.: IVP, 1976.
W. Berns, *For Capital Punishment*. New York: Basic Books, 1979.
C. S. Lewis, *God in the Dock: Essays on Theology and Ethics*. Ed. W. Hooper. Grand Rapids: Eerdmans, 1970, pp. 287-300.
G. McHugh, *Christian Faith and Criminal Justice*. New York: Paulist Press, 1978.

7

Euthanasia:
When Is Enough Enough?

THOUGH SHE LIES QUIETLY IN a coma, Karen Ann Quinlan has spoken eloquently to the whole world about the meaning of life and death. The decision rendered in March 1976 by Chief Justice Richard J. Hughes of the New Jersey Supreme Court was greeted by cheers and boos. The heart of the decision gave Miss Quinlan's father, Joseph, guardianship of his daughter's person. The decision included the understanding that the Quinlan family, the attending physician and the ethics committee of the hospital had the authority together to decide to remove the respirator that had sustained Miss Quinlan's life for about four years.

Her case poses the question of whether medical authorities always have the obligation to prolong life even when hope for meaningful recovery has long since vanished. By his verdict, spelled out in a fifty-nine page decision, Chief Justice Hughes indicated that biological existence is not all that there is to human living. People who seek to live by God's Word would certainly agree with that conclusion and would do well to think through and to mine out the biblical principles at stake in decisions like the Quinlan case.

If her tragic story were an isolated case we might ignore it and go on to other issues. But virtually all intensive care units in North America could tell similar stories. People whose brains are damaged beyond recovery are kept alive with pumps, tubes and wires, while distraught relatives and perplexed physicians ponder their responsibilities. When is enough enough?

Euthanasia is a word whispered in hospital corridors. What does it mean? How should we feel about it? Literally, euthanasia means "good death," but the Greek roots could be better paraphrased as "easy death" or "death that is encouraged to curtail suffering." As is often the case with ethical and political dilemmas, the Bible does not give us much direct and specific help. Instead we have to dig out principles and guidelines from biblical teaching in general. In so doing, it may be helpful to distinguish between *passive* euthanasia, in which medical or mechanical means are withheld from use to prolong life and *active* euthanasia, in which medication might be prescribed to hasten death in painful and irrecoverable illnesses.

Passive Euthanasia

As Christians we have an *obligation to promote human life*. We know where it comes from and why it is important, so our bias is always in favor of life. For this reason, we hate war, even when it may be necessary, are fearful of abortion on demand and may support capital punishment as the ultimate way to demonstrate how serious it is to tamper with people created by God.

We remember how Jesus promoted life by the miracles that he wrought when he lived among us. He showed no class preference: he raised from the dead the son of a poor widow in Nain and the daughter of an influential ruler named Jairus. He healed the centurion's servant whom he had never seen and the mother-in-law of Peter who was soon to be a close friend. He was the resurrection and the life at work among us. From him we learn the value of life. The defeat of disease and death was one of the proofs that the kingdom had come. We as sons and daughters of that kingdom continue to rejoice in that victory and enter into it with a war against illness.

We also remember that our doctrine of creation encourages us to use all God-ordained means to promote life: hygiene, sanitation, nutrition, medication, technology and surgery. The discoveries of how our bodies work and what will promote health and healing have to be viewed as gifts of the Creator who works in orderly fashion and helps us comprehend how he works.

We further remember that the Bible's teaching on resurrection tells us how important our bodies are. No doctrine of salvation is complete without the restoration of our bodies from the damage done by death and illness. God's plan from the beginning was our wholeness—body and spirit. The resurrection will see to that.

Because of all that we believe about Jesus' miracles, God's creation and the coming resurrection, we have the obligation to promote human life. Whatever plagues, abuses or corrupts the human body is our enemy.

Promoting human life is one thing; prolonging it is another. As Christians we have the *option of prolonging human life*, so long as that life can be truly human. On biblical terms, true humanity means the possibility of enjoying worship of God and fellowship with one another. If human life is more than mere biological life, then vital signs like pulse and respiration are not all that living entails. On the other hand achievement and productivity are not necessary for life to be human—not in the way that prayer and love are.

In other words, where accident or irreversible disease make it impossible for a human being to worship God or give and receive love, our task is to make that person as comfortable as possible as long as the person's own life support system will sustain her or him. Once the inevitability of death and the inability of the person to experience life's great purposes become clear, we as Christians have every obligation to minister in love, but no obligation to use extraordinary means to prolong life.

This is sometimes called passive euthanasia. Practiced with the love and care outlined above, I believe it is fully in accord with the teachings of God's Word. Of course, love will insist: (1) that as much objective evidence as can reasonably be known about the degree of damage, especially to the brain, and about the impossibility of recovery will be taken into consideration; (2) that the decision will be made in terms of the patient's welfare, not the convenience of those who are to care for him or her; (3) that those consulted in the decision will be those who care most about the patient and are committed to his or her welfare; and (4) that the entire matter will be made the subject of fervent, careful investigation of the medical facts, and diligent heart searching to make sure our motives meet God's approval.

Our doctrine of eternal fellowship with God is significant to this discussion. Death is an enemy, but a vanquished one. Whatever mysteries death may hold, whatever terrors we feel as we face it, it does not have the last word, let alone the last laugh. God is there to welcome his children home. When our biological processes no longer have meaning, there will yet be substance to our lives in fellowship with God: "For to me to live is Christ, and to die is gain" (Phil. 1:21). When is enough enough? When God says, "Enough!" Then his enough will lead to more than we have dreamed possible.

Active Euthanasia

There may be relatively little debate among Christian believers about what I have said thus far. Where the going gets rough is when we move from the possibility of passive euthanasia to the committing of active euthanasia.

As Christians, we believe that God has come to us in Jesus; therefore, *we must refuse to play God*. As with abortion, so with euthanasia: we must refrain from destroying what we cannot create. None of us can replicate that great act at history's beginning: "then the LORD God formed man of dust from the ground, and breathed into his nostrils the breath of life; and man became a living being" (Gen. 2:7). Mold the dust as you will and puff into it as you please, but nothing will result save scattered dust, some of which will lodge in your eye. Let it be a lesson in learning the difference between you and God. A secular world may be increasingly willing to say who should live and when we should die; Christians read such decisions as brash at best and blasphemous at worst.

As Christians, we believe in the human propensity toward sin. This means that *we must guard against all possible abuse* in matters of life and death. In decisions about active euthanasia, our governments and courts are bound to become involved. Decisions may be perverted or manipulated. Motives may turn sour. Yet the decision is irreversible; the mistake, if it proves to be one, is uncorrectable.

As Christians, we believe that God made every person, even those irrecoverably maimed or incapacitated, in his image. This means that *we must treasure human uniqueness*. They shoot horses whose broken legs render them not only painfully uncomfortable but also totally unproductive. We must not treat people the same way. When biology and structure fail, an animal may have lost all meaning; a person has not. Since we do not know all that goes on in the inner self of a suffering person, we do not have the right to put that person out of suffering, though we may have the obligation to work for the least distress possible.

Active euthanasia? The answer seems to be no for those who hold to the beliefs and values taught in the sacred Book. The responsibility is too great to be safe in human hands; the decision is too ultimate to be trusted to our incomplete and fallen human ingenuity.

Guidelines for Living with the Difficulty

Voting yes on passive euthanasia and no on active does not allow us to brush the dust of the matter off our hands and stride merrily on our way. The problems will yet be there: women in comas, whose brains seem destroyed but whose vital signs pulse on with the sturdiness of an athlete; men whose organs are being consumed with cancer till the pain is beyond dulling; children with congenital defects that an earlier generation would have displayed in sideshows. Whatever else fails in wisdom and understanding, our compassion must not wane. The problems are many, vexing and painful. Clustered around each of these problems are persons for whom the bedside is a Gethsemane: doctors, nurses, hospital administrators and staff, and loved ones. "When is enough enough?" they cry out. We must do more than answer, "Not yet."

At a most practical level, *we must share the cost of prolonged care*. This may mean paying our insurance premiums and our taxes cheerfully, knowing that one use of them is help for the helpless. Beyond that, doing what we can may mean contributing of our own means to help sustain financially those who cannot help themselves. Our own and our churches' stewardship may need to make room for this need. If human life is as valuable as we preach, we may have to put our money where our mouths are.

Again at the practical level, *we must exhibit stead-*

fastness in love. Prolonged illness saps the energies of love as almost nothing else can. The more handicapped the person, the greater the toll of love: the needs are more; the rewards are fewer. How many of us will make it part of our Christian ministry to bring the Savior's love to those maimed and battered spirits whom life has deprived of the privileges of normal activity? An enterprising Californian has recruited and trained a cadre of persons to sit with the dying who have no companions. Friendship for hire! It would be unnecessary if we who shout so loudly about life's sanctity paid a higher price to express love to what we deem sacred.

In the face of prolonged and puzzling suffering, *we must have patience to accept the mystery*. The what and why of God's ways are beyond our reach. Our question marks are never bent with more violence nor dotted with more ferocity than when we look at life's casualty list. All explanations turn to chalk in our throats. What is God up to? He treats people so differently that if one of us did what he does we would brand the practice unfair. So with pain for the sufferer's plight and with frustration over our own ignorance, we serve while we wait.

Yet despite the hard questions, *we must have confidence that God is present*. No visiting hours restrict his entry; no forbidding nurses with arched brows ease him from the sickroom. God is present and at work. He is at work in the love and care of those who tend the helplessly and hopelessly infirm. At times, he has healed those whose clinical symptoms rattled with death. Who is to say that he cannot communicate to the inner recesses of persons beyond our reach? What messages of love and care does he whisper to ears thought deaf? What works of goodness does he purpose through suffering, even when that suffering seems outrageous?

We are all more than our symptoms. When our biology has collapsed, there is still an "us" that God loves and cares for. The Bible speaks of realities of life and love that chemistry cannot analyze. When suffering is at its worst, we must be most convinced of these realities. When we are, Paul's text will become ours: "Yes, and I shall rejoice. For I know that through your prayers and the help of the Spirit of Jesus Christ this will turn out for my deliverance, as it is my eager expectation and hope that I shall not be at all ashamed, but that with full courage now as always Christ will be honored in my body, whether by life or by death" (Phil. 1:19-20).

For further reading

N. Anderson, *Issues of Life and Death*. Downers Grove, Ill.: IVP, 1976.

R. Kopp, *Encounter With Terminal Illness*. Grand Rapids: Zondervan, 1980.

R. Ramsey, *Ethic at the Edges of Life: Medical and Legal Intersections*. New Haven: Yale Univ. Press, 1978.

F. Schaeffer and C. E. Koop, *Whatever Happened to the Human Race?* Old Tappan, N.J.: Revell, 1979.

J. Shelly, *Dilemma: A Nurse's Guide for Making Ethical Decisions*. Downers Grove, Ill.: IVP, 1980.

8

Civil Disobedience:

What If the Law Seems Wrong?

I HOPE WE NEVER SEE THOSE days again. The very memory of them makes my stomach turn. Helmeted policemen bearing hardwood clubs in one hand and plastic shields in the other advanced steadily toward the mobs of angry students. The air reeked with obscenities and tear gas. The atmosphere was explosive with anger.

The days that I hope never to see again were the tumultuous sixties when the generation gap widened to a gaping gulf, when establishments of all kinds were pressured to change, when the very foundations of our law and order were sent rocking.

Those vicious, vexing days seem far behind us now. Establishments have learned to change, at least on occasion; parents have attempted to listen to the longings of their children, at least in some instances; those responsible for making and enforcing our laws do seem more sensitive, at least when we are able to get their attention. Above all, our student generation has learned to make its point by less threatening ways than sit-ins, less vicious ways than burning buildings, less harmful ways than assaulting police. The tragedy of Kent State University may have been a turning point. Structures of power have learned less violent ways of coping with dissent, and the younger generation has learned the cost of defying the laws of the land.

Christians must look at questions of obeying or disobeying laws through two sets of lenses. We are citizens of lands, governed by constitutions and laws. Part of our Christian responsibility is to have respect for the laws of our land, since we know that civil government plays a God-given role: "Let every person be subject to the governing authorities. For there is no authority except from God, and those that exist have been instituted by God" (Rom. 13:1).

Yet we are also citizens of a new kingdom. Our motto—no, more than that—our confession is "Jesus is Lord." Ultimately all kingdoms will belong to him. We are his obedient subjects called and empowered to live his kind of life.

Given these two lenses through which we look at law and government, conflict is inevitable. True, in a democracy there will probably be less conflict than where authority is more oppressive and power is more concentrated. But as long as we and those who govern us are fallen creatures, no government will totally conform to the standards of Christ's kingdom. In the best earthly place you can imagine, there is still a gap between the way in which God's will is *not* done on earth and the way it *is* done in heaven.

When that gap becomes critical enough and large enough, Christians face a terrifying decision. Which citizenship takes priority? How can I live responsibly within my earthly kingdom and still be fully loyal to that kingdom above where Christ is Lord? If the law seems wrong, what do I do about it?

Biblical Patterns

Happily the Bible is not silent on such questions. For more than three thousand years it has been mindful of the potential conflict between the arbitrary decisions of human governors and the will of God.

The two pivotal events of the Bible—Israel's exodus from Egypt and Jesus' resurrection from the dead— were acts of God that defied the authority of government. Though Pharaoh gave permission for Israel to migrate from Egypt, battered as he was by the plagues, he later changed his mind and pursued them. In Egypt, Pharaoh was the law. His word had absolute authority since he was viewed as the incarnation of the sun god, Ra. Yet his orders for the Israelites to return and his commands to his troops to head off their escape were countermanded by the call of God. In response to the command of the Lord, the Israelites dramatically and flagrantly broke the laws of Egypt.

Matthew's account of Christ's resurrection needs no explanation:

> The chief priests and the Pharisees gathered before Pilate and said, "Sir, we remember how that imposter said, while he was still alive, 'After three days I will rise again.' Therefore order the sepulchre to be made secure until the third day, lest his disciples go and steal him away, and tell the people, 'He has risen from the dead,' and the last fraud will be worse than the first." Pilate said to them, "You have a guard of soldiers; go, make it as secure as you can." So they went and made the sepulchre secure by sealing the stone and setting a guard. (Mt. 27:62-66)

God had other plans: the seal was broken; the stone removed; the guard confounded; the body raised. The two kingdoms had clashed, and the heavenly one was the winner.

Some of the Bible's outstanding figures challenged the authority of the governments that in their day held sway. Daniel willfully transgressed the laws of the Medes and Persians that forbade prayer to anyone save King Darius: "When Daniel knew that the document had been signed, he went to his house where he had windows in his upper chamber open toward Jerusalem; and he got down upon his knees three times a day and prayed and gave thanks before his God, as he had done previously" (Dan. 6:10). Every Sunday-school child knows the outcome: Daniel's arrest, the lions' den, the divine deliverance. The law was clear, but so was Daniel's utter defiance of it.

With Peter, the situation was no different. In his case the authorities were the "rulers and elders and scribes" (Acts 4:5), the cream of religious leadership in Jerusalem. "So they [these religious rulers] called them [Peter and John] and charged them not to speak or teach at all in the name of Jesus. But Peter and John answered them, 'Whether it is right in the sight of God to listen to you rather than to God, you must judge; for we cannot but speak of what we have seen and heard' " (Acts 4:18-20). Speak they did—so much so that most of the apostles paid with their lives for the persistence with which they obeyed God.

Practical Concerns

The biblical pattern is plain: there are times when the people of God must violate human laws in order to do the will of God. But the Bible by no means gives us a blank check to become lawbreakers! There are some highly practical concerns that God's men and women keep in mind when faced with seeming conflicts between God's Word and man's rules.

Be sure the concern is biblical. Careful testing of the issues involved is essential. Partisan causes and momentary grievances can assume monumental proportions when we are hurt by the workings of government. Even our consciences, valuable as they are, can misdirect us to rash behavior. The same is true of the opinions of well-meaning people. When laws pinch, everything within us wriggles for freedom.

Search the Scriptures—that must be the motto on such occasions. Search the whole Scripture, not just the parts that seem to support your viewpoint. Search the Scriptures, and consult with other mature Christians to learn their interpretation and application of God's Word.

Where God's commands to love and worship him are violated by any laws, this issue is clear. With Peter and Daniel we must listen to God, not men. Where freedom of worship is restricted, where the state or its head is made the object of worship, we have no choice but to disobey that law. The lordship of Christ and our higher citizenship in his kingdom demand it.

But what about other commands of God such as the law to love our neighbors? What should be our response if the state asks us to deal unjustly or cruelly with others? Here the matter may not be so clear.

We may all agree that Hitler's subordinates should have refused to obey the orders that claimed the lives of six million Jews. After all, that was murder, a bold and blatant breach of the Ten Commandments. But what about the violence done to human rights and dignity by laws that for years required some American citizens to ride in the back of the bus? Where was our regard for the law of neighborly love at that time? Was not the law of God, the golden rule, in head-on conflict with local laws in some of our cities? Or take the case of my California neighbors who were Japanese. What protest did I and my Christian friends raise when, without trial or hearings, they were taken by the thousands with a handful of personal effects and held in relocation camps after Pearl Harbor? At that point national security and personal safety became more important to us than the law of God. Was that right? Were we truly obedient to the Bible when we let such things happen without interceding for those who were suffering abuse?

Be sure all legal efforts have been exhausted before you consider breaking a law that conflicts with the Word of God. One of the great strengths of our democratic processes is the opportunity they give us to change what is not right in our governments. Bad laws can be challenged in the courts. Wicked lawmakers can be thrust from office by recall elections.

Dishonest judges or lawyers can be disciplined by the bar associations. Brutal police can be brought to trial before police commissions.

For Christians, defying civil law is never a trivial matter. We can consider it only when we are convinced that all legitimate efforts to bring change have failed. God's Word tells us that his people must obey him under all circumstances, even where such obedience puts us in conflict with human law. But God's Word also tells us that human law is itself very important to God. We can only decide to violate it when all peaceful, lawful attempts to alter the matter have been tested.

Finally, and this is of vital importance, *be sure to submit to the law* even when the Bible and the circumstances persuade you that the law must be broken. Christians who with great soul-searching sense the need to defy a given law do not become outlaws. Anarchistic, violent lawlessness is not a Christian endeavor. Even revolution, in those rare instances when it becomes necessary, must be lamented in the name of law. Anarchists will use revolution to their own gain. God-fearing revolutionaries will challenge the established order because they want to impose higher, better laws.

Submitting to law, even as we break it, means using means as lawful as possible to bring the needed change. That was one of the great strengths of the nonviolence employed during the civil-rights movement of the sixties. It rewrote bad laws not by bloody violence but by passive resistance that sought to remain as loving as possible.

Submitting to law also means that we have to be willing to take the penalty to which Christian civil disobedience may lead. Daniel, Peter and Paul all faced imprisonment, even martyrdom, at the hands of civil governments. If the Bible so lights our consciences that we see clearly the need to resist a specific law of our government, we must do so with the willing recognition that the government has a right to punish us for our disobedience.

No government does everything right. But if governments are to play their God-given role, which is "to punish those who do wrong and to praise those who do right" (1 Pet. 2:14), then they must have the right to enforce their laws. Christians in many times and many places have not shied away from martyrdom when they heard God's Word speaking clearly to their consciences.

I hope we never see those harrowing scenes of the sixties again. Confrontation with government can be a painful, embittering experience, especially for a Christian. But if the time comes when local, state or federal law forces us to do what the Bible forbids, we must be ready to make the right choice. We must be ready to choose against the government for the sake of government. Our civil disobedience, if and when it takes place, must be aimed to make bad government better. It must also be aimed to support Christ's kingdom of love and righteousness to which all of God's people pledge daily allegiance.

For further reading

D. Kaufman, *What Belongs To Caeser?* Scottdale, Pa.: Herald Press, 1969.

M. King, *Where Do We Go From Here?* New York: Harper & Row, 1967.

R. Linder and R. Pierard, *Twilight of the Saints*. Downers Grove, Ill.: IVP, 1978.

R. Sider, *Christ and Violence*. Scottdale, Pa.: Herald Press, 1979.

9

Ecology:

How Careful Should We Be of Our Environment?

THE SUBJECT AT THE ROUND luncheon table had switched to cars, more specifically to the gasoline mileage that various models achieve. I suggested that most of us ought to drive smaller cars to cut down our fuel consumption and to save irreplaceable resources of energy. I was taken aback more than slightly when one of my table mates scoffed at the whole idea of an energy crisis, branding it a deceptive plot perpetrated against the people by the petroleum industry. "Why," he pontificated, "we have enough petroleum to last us for a couple of hundred more years."

That conversation, in slightly altered form, has rattled the cups on thousands of tables, round and square, rectangular and oval, in the restaurants of the Western world. It reminds us of several important issues that we face. Precisely what is the reserve of natural resources available to us? How rapidly do we dare use known supplies when there is so much that we do not know about the supply and demand for resources? What is a fair distribution of resources between those who have them and those who do not? If an essential resource is found within the boundaries of one nation and not of others, does that nation have the right to use all of it for its own purposes? What is our responsibility to generations to come? Can we deplete the supply of fossil fuel now, for instance, and allow later generations to fend for themselves? Incredibly difficult questions these are, sufficiently complex to engage our conversations through a millennium of luncheons.

Christians cannot duck them simply because they are difficult. After all, the resources we are talking about, the environment we live in and the world that depends on those resources are all the work of God. They were all ordered and sustained by God for his purpose. That was why he called them "good" at the beginning. "Good" means right for his purposes and precisely what he intended as part of his creative plan.

A Biblical View of the Environment

Christians, therefore, have a large stake in ecology, the study of relationships between life forms in our environment. Our reasons for concern are not just *romantic*. There have been those, especially in the first half of the 1800s, who fell in love with nature—its beauty, its power, its vitality, its self-sufficiency. Novelists, painters, poets and naturalists treasured the earth as though it were a goddess from whom they sought both love and nurture. People who take their cues from the Bible know the difference between the creation and the Creator. Their adoration goes to the Lord of the universe, not to the universe. They are not romantics, but they do have great respect for the works of God's hands.

We are also different in our concerns from *religious mystics*. The influence of Eastern, especially Buddhist, thought on views of ecology has been prominent in recent years. To these modern mystics humanity is such an intimate part of the universe that true meaning and true repose are found in meditation on our oneness with the world. People for whom the Bible is God's unerring Word will not join these mystic meditators. We understand that human beings are creatures of God but creatures different from the rest of the creation, creatures made to love and worship God, creatures with greater privilege and greater responsibility than the animals, vegetables and minerals that surround and sustain us.

Finally, we are different from those who relate to the world as *exploiters*. That word describes those for whom the creation exists to supply their needs and, especially, to satisfy their greed. They see all earth's resources as gold for hoarding, fuel for gobbling or trinkets for amusement. The exploiters may be hedonists who live for sheer pleasure or industrialists whose game is power. Christian men and women should not attend to their amusement or join their games. Our view of the universe is far more serious than the most ardent exploiters can ever know.

How careful should we be of our environment? We should be as careful of it as God was when he created it, and we should be mindful of the reasons for such care. Ecology is not a peripheral subject, not an elective course, for those who love and serve God as Creator. Our care for the environment is part of our God-given urge for survival, part of our God-ordered expression of worship, part of our God-commanded participation in service.

An Urge for Survival

As a book of history and prophecy, the Bible takes us from the creation of the world to the Second Coming of Christ, which will result in a new heaven and a new earth. How long this period will stretch we do not know. We have no firm date for history's beginning; likewise, no person, not even Jesus himself in his earthly stay, could know the hour when the Son of man will come again. This we do know: when God created our spinning planet he intended it to keep going as long as it suited his purposes. The survival of life on earth, life with the quality that God designed, is not merely a social or scientific question; it is clearly a theological matter.

The human family has an urge for survival *in response to God's purpose*. We cannot listen to the creation story too frequently. More than any other part of the Bible it reminds us of why we are here:

> So God created man in his own image, in the image of God he created him; male and female he created them. And God blessed them, and God said to them, "Be fruitful and multiply, and fill the earth and subdue it; and have dominion over the fish of the sea and over the birds of the air and over every

living thing that moves upon the earth." And God said, "Behold, I have given you every plant yielding seed which is upon the face of all the earth, and every tree with seed in its fruit; you shall have them for food. And to every beast of the earth, and to every bird of the air, and to everything that creeps on the earth, everything that has the breath of life, I have given every green plant for food." And it was so. And God saw everything that he had made, and behold, it was very good. And there was evening and there was morning, a sixth day. (Gen. 1:27-31)

One of God's great purposes in creation was survival; therefore, the human family was to multiply to assure that survival. We were also to use our God-given talents (part of the gift of being created in God's image) to "have dominion over" the rest of creation—responsibility for the survival of what God has made. We and the animal world were given herbs, grain and fruit to sustain us as part of that program. All of this God called very good. So one human task is to care for what God has made until all his purposes are fulfilled when Christ comes again. God wants a cared-for world and an obedient human family as tributes to his glory. We need improvement on both counts.

An Expression of Worship

Ecology, our concern for the home that God framed and furnished for us, should also be an expression of worship. In purest and simplest terms, our environment—air to breathe, earth to till, water to refresh us, light for growth, beauty to enjoy, creatures to study—is *a gift of God*.

Esteem for the Giver must mean appreciation for

the gifts. What items among your possessions do you value most? Not necessarily the most expensive nor the most artistic ones. The treasured, cherished items are those given by the people whom you most honor. That is one of the great attractions of heirlooms. I wear on my little finger a simple gold band. It would win no prizes at an exhibition; it would command, if sold, only the price of the few grains of gold that comprise it. But I cherish it, wear it daily, fondle it frequently. It was my mother's wedding ring, and I prize it because of my esteem for her.

In much the same way, the world around us may not seem all that we would wish it to be, but we must treat it as something awesomely precious. It comes to us from the hand and by the word of the king of the universe. It is not to be trifled with.

Ecology may also be an expression of worship when we realize that the entire universe was created *in praise of God.* In other words, our environment is not only God's gift, designed to assure our survival as we carry out his purpose. Our environment is also God's instrument, designed to celebrate his glory:

The heavens are telling the glory of God;
and the firmament proclaims his handiwork.
(Ps. 19:1)

God's people will resist any use of those heavens and that firmament which would muffle creation's song of glory.

A Participation in Service

God wills our survival in order that his purposes may reach their grand climax in Christ's coming. God wants our worship as we value his gifts in the world around us and as we celebrate the praise they render to him. God also insists that we, as members of the human family, participate in his mission of making his glory known on earth as it is in heaven.

Our care for his creation and especially for human beings as the crown of his creation—our ecology, in other words—is part of that mission. Tilling the ground, managing the land and its resources, and helping God's creation survive and thrive are truly human and fully Christian tasks. God's commitment from the beginning has been to human wholeness and human welfare. We are called by him to share that commitment.

Ecology, of course, is no substitute for evangelism. The core of our Christian mission worldwide is to present Jesus Christ as God's Son and our Savior, calling men and women to repentance from sin, to faith in him and to responsible partnership in God's family, the church. Yet ecology and evangelism are tied together in Scripture itself: "For the creation waits with eager longing for the revealing of the sons of God; for the creation was subjected to futility, not of its own will but by the will of him who subjected it in hope; because the creation itself will be set free from its bondage to decay and obtain the glorious liberty of the children of God" (Rom. 8:19-21).

Creation, since human sin first stunned and shattered Eden's bliss, has not been what it ought to be. Nor will it be truly whole, entirely good, until God's redemptive purpose is fulfilled and the task of world evangelization is completed. Then creation will enjoy the freedom to fulfill God's intention to the utmost. The very heavens and earth will be blessed as men and women everywhere come to confess Jesus as Lord and Savior.

The God who cared enough to create and sustain, the God who will care enough to free his creation from "bondage to decay," surely cares for it along the way. More than that, he calls us to do the same.

Ecological interest should be more than the fad of a few conservationists; it should not be left to the romantics and mystics among us. Ecology is of both practical and profound Christian concern.

If human survival is important to God, then pollution of our waters is an offense. If our worship is vital to God, who framed the heavens as a gift to us and praise to him, then smog is an abomination. If our service is commanded by him, then the ruthless exploitation and consumption of our resources is a reproach to his name.

How much fuel do we have to fire the engines of civilization? How much dare we use in our affluent lands? How much ought we to spare for tomorrow's generations? These are not casual questions to occupy the lunch hour. They are matters of passionate spiritual concern. Christian discipleship means dealing with them in the name of the Lord of all, who is our Creator and Redeemer.

For further reading
B. Jackson, *Only One Earth: The Care and Maintenance of a Small Planet*. New York: Norton, 1972.
J. Rogers, *Ecological Theology*. Kampen: Kok, 1973.
D. Slusser, *Technology: The God that Failed*. Philadelphia: Westminster, 1971.

10

Consumerism:

How Can I Get My Money's Worth?

IT HAS BECOME A REGULAR part of the nightly newscast. There he sits beside the anchorman and anchorwoman, the sportscaster, the weather reporter and the movie reviewer. Each evening he takes his five minutes to address his subject; all day he works with his staff to prepare it. His presence is something new and something welcome in our society.

He is the consumer expert, the latest addition to those massive crews that keep us in touch with the happenings of our city and our world. His assignments have been legion. Night by night he asks the viewers to send in their complaints of shoddy treatment by the businesses of the community, and day by day he and his team write or phone to investigate the grievances and to get them redressed when they can.

He is a powerful person. Managers of firms who have been at fault know that their mistakes, unkindnesses and inefficiencies may become household knowledge to hundreds of thousands if their names are mentioned on the tube. The results obtained by our consumer expert are impressive. Hundreds of viewers have had damaged goods replaced or ill-spent money refunded because of his labors.

It is probably an overstatement to say, as one of our late presidents did, that the business of America is business. But there is enough truth in the statement to remind us that our society is highly dependent on business transactions. Most North Americans neither manufacture any of the goods that they use nor grow any of the food that they consume. Instead we render services to others. Secretaries, gardeners, carpenters, lawyers, computer programmers, physicians, truck drivers and preachers—we all help to meet the needs of other people, trading our time and skill for their money. In turn, we trade that money for the food and goods which others produce and which sustain our lives.

Those who buy our specialized services count on us for competence and efficiency. We who buy the goods and food of others count on them for quality and reliability. Business in one form or another is essential to all of us; the way businesses are conducted directly affects each of us. I welcome, therefore, our local consumer expert and am pleased to note that this breed is increasing across the land so that virtually every major newspaper and many radio stations offer a similar service.

A Precedent from the Prophets

In biblical days, the prophets of God sometimes served as consumer experts. Amos, for example, had a watchful eye for crooked business practices:

> Hear this, you who trample upon the needy,
>   and bring the poor of the land to an end,
> saying, "When will the new moon be over,
>   that we may sell grain?
> And the sabbath,
>   that we may offer wheat for sale,
> that we may make the ephah small and the
>   shekel great,
>   and deal deceitfully with false balances,
> that we may buy the poor for silver
>   and the needy for a pair of sandals,
>   and sell the refuse of the wheat?"
> (Amos 8:4-6)

Ralph Nader's criticisms of some of our modern business practices seem bland beside Amos's exposé.

Greed is the clue to the problem. The Israelites to whom the prophet spoke 750 years before Christ were thoroughly greedy: (1) they could not wait for the sacred holidays to end, so eager were they to get on with their sharp trading; (2) they cheated on their weights (the *shekel* was the weight used to balance the scale) and their measures (the *ephah* was the container for measuring grain) and (3) they tricked their consumers by selling the chaff, husks and probably some dust along with the wheat. Their greed was so aggressive that they were willing to see people starve or be sold into slavery for the sake of monetary gain.

God-fearing citizens like the prophets were to aid the helpless poor, whose limitations were pitiful. They could travel only as far for food as they could walk. The number of grain venders in any one market would have been few, preventing competition which helps insure honesty. They had few means of storing or preserving food so they were continually dependent on the merchants. There were no regulatory agencies monitoring the transactions to assure justice.

By each of the criteria above most of us are better off, but there is still no room for complacency. False packaging, price fixing, substandard products (including dirty grain), inflated prices for the poor, high-pressure sales tactics—these and a long list of other wrongs can be documented every year in our society.

This is as relevant to the Christian in the twentieth century after Christ as it was to the prophet of God in the eighth century before Christ. *The essentials are the same:* greed is a common human trait; some people are more powerful or more affluent or more clever than others; greed often prompts those who possess power, wealth or shrewdness to take advantage of those who do not.

Most important, *God's concern is the same.* The goods and food which we consume are all his. We manufacture, grow, transport and sell; he alone creates. But even more importantly, the people who buy and sell are responsible to him. He is their Creator and Lord. They did not just appear on earth by some chancy process of evolution; they were created and placed here by him. His care and concern brought them and keeps them here.

Keeping our businesses as honest as possible,

therefore, is not just the task of edgy, angry, young experts. It is the responsibility of all of us who believe what the Bible teaches about stewardship and love.

An Expression of Stewardship

Working for sound business practices is part of our duty as *stewards of God's money*. Allowing ourselves to be cheated or defrauded without protest is irresponsible. What we have is a gift of God—a gift he expects us to use wisely.

This is not easy in a world which is part foolish and part selfish. One host of us is willing to be fooled and another host is equally willing to do the fooling. It is an outrageous form of the law of supply and demand. The demand for foolish trinkets, for impossible bargains, for something for almost nothing, for what looks like a steal is so persistent that manufacturers and merchants wrack their brains trying to supply that demand.

Christian stewards ought to know better. We should watch what we buy, how much we pay for it and how well we use it. Our discipleship insists on this. We must give no encouragement to venders who sell goods of quality, durability and usefulness below the value reflected in the price.

Christians see the human family as *stewards of God's resources* as well as of his money. This means that wastefulness is to be avoided. Our raw materials need to be put to their best use. Resources hard to replace must not be consumed for frivolity or for profit alone. They must always be seen as a means to service. The good of the human family should be the aim of our businesses, not merely the profit of the stockholders. Profit there must be, of course, or there will be no businesses to serve us. But the service, not the profit, must be the chief aim. Any other attitude results in a dangerously complacent or a wickedly selfish use of God-given resources. The dreadful example of the buffalo hunters of the Great Plains a century ago serves as a painful reminder of how God's goods can be scornfully squandered by people who do not live as stewards.

A Demonstration of Love

In a world both careless and angry, love is in strong demand, though not in high supply. One way in which love can be demonstrated is for God's people to protect the disadvantaged against exploitation. Our laws have helped in this area: food and drugs are monitored for quality and harmlessness; offerings of stocks and bonds are controlled to guard against swindles; professional standards for doctors, lawyers, dentists, architects, engineers and psychologists are regulated by governmental agencies and professional associations; educational institutions are evaluated for effectiveness and stability by accrediting associations; the gallons on our gas pumps and the pounds (soon to be kilograms) on our food scales are certified by the proper bureaus. These are acts of love, though legal technicalities and bureaucratic excesses may sometimes keep them from working that way.

And yet there is work for God's people to do. Minorities often must pay higher prices than others do for what they buy, especially if they live in areas where there are fewer stores from which to choose. Credit for them is more difficult to establish, making them vulnerable to loan sharks who demand outrageous interest from desperate people.

All of us are susceptible to the lures of powerful advertising. Products are called "better" or "best" with no measurable evidence behind the claim. Brands gain prominence more from media ballyhoo than from their intrinsic quality. Children and teenagers are manipulated into using worthless products or eating junk food by the omnipresent commercial. Consumerism can be an expression of Christian love when pressure is applied to protect the gullible and the unwary among us from the fraudulent and the harmful.

Such pressure, exerted with fairness and based on facts, can be an act of love toward those who are taking advantage of others. They may need to realize what they are doing when they act in ignorance, unmindful that their product is harmful. Think how many well-meaning people sold refined sugar before we discovered the problems it may cause.

Fair-minded confrontation can help offenders change their ways. They need to know where they are wrong to rid themselves of guilt which they carry if they are deliberately deceiving people and to avoid the judgment which God will impose on those who abuse his creation. Amos, the great consumer advocate, was well aware of that judgment:

> The LORD has sworn by the pride of Jacob [that is, by his own name]:
> "Surely I will never forget any of their deeds.
> Shall not the land tremble on this account...?"
> (Amos 8:7-8)

An expression of stewardship of God's money and God's resources, a demonstration of love for the abused and the abusers—these are biblical responsibilities. There also are basic guidelines for strengthening the integrity and enlarging the effectiveness of our nations' businesses.

We must give quality service in all our work. Most of us contribute in some way to our national productivity. We are producers of food, services or goods. If the whole population did its work as well as we do ours, what would be the effect? Improvement? I hope so.

We must insist on value in return for our money. Products must be as close to what they claim to be as human skill can make them. This insistence is hard work. It means taking things back, registering complaints, arguing with clerks, straightening out computer mistakes and, perhaps, refusing to pay. But we must do what we can. Unscrupulous people count on our complacency. We should not let them win because when they do, the whole community loses, including the unscrupulous purveyors of shoddy merchandise. We may even need to write to the consumer expert on the evening newscast, if we cannot satisfy our grievance any other way.

We must let honesty work against us as well as for us. Consumer greed is no more godly than producer greed. Do we pay our bills promptly and keep our contracts squarely? Do we return the extra change to the clerk who made a sleepy mistake? Do we correct the waitress when she leaves out an item on our dinner check?

Discipleship takes seriously all of these obligations. It believes that God is ultimately as interested in the quality of our business life as he is in the quality of our church life. All of life is his; we want to heed his call to live it both responsibly and abundantly.

For further reading
D. Hessel, *Energy Ethics*. New York: Friendship Press, 1979.
D. Shriver, Jr., *Rich Man Poor Man*. Richmond: John Knox Press, 1972.
R. Sider, ed., *Living More Simply: Biblical Principles and Practical Models*. Downers Grove, Ill.: IVP, 1980.

Affluence:

Why Can't I Spend What's Mine?

THE SUPERMARKET TELLS THE story. Its aisles are piled high with cans, jars and packages. The pickle shelves alone are forbidding: dill, sweet, watermelon, cucumber, bread and butter; gherkins, chips, relishes; pickled beets, pickled carrots, pickled peppers, pickled cauliflower; half a hundred products from a dozen companies... and all for garnish.

If the pickle shelves are forbidding, the soap and detergent counter is intimidating. Brands shout their names in blue, red, yellow, orange and black letters, each hollering louder than the other its claims to cleansing power. Powders, pellets, flakes, sprays and liquids clutch at your sleeve as you stroll by, tugging for a chance to leap from the shelf into your shopping cart.

The supermarket tells the story of our affluence. From pickles to detergents, from crackers to cereals—and what a wheaty, sugary, crunchy display that is in our market—from juices to jams, from meats to cheeses, from produce to beverages, the supermarket tells the story of our affluence. Never has a society had more to choose from at prices more affordable than ours. Based on national averages, we citizens of the United States and Canada spend a smaller percentage of our income for food than virtually any people, past or present, in the world.

The supermarket shelves are a symbol of our affluence. Behind them are the storerooms, warehouses, frozen food lockers and silos of our lands, teeming with the fruit of our labors and the gifts of our God. And all this has to do with groceries only. What about the rich deposits of coal and oil shale? What about the massive reserves of natural gas and oil? What about the generous stands of timber? What about the fields that overflow with cotton? What about the giant rivers and countless lakes that supply our water? What about the humming factories that turn out thousands of products for our convenience and comfort?

Affluent is an adjective descriptive of our society, though not equally of everyone within it. We see great economic differences between the wealthy of our spacious suburbs and the unemployed young men of our crowded ghettos. But when people from outside North America look at our way of life, they consider almost all of us affluent. The poorest among us look rich to the thousands of men and women who sleep on the sidewalks of Calcutta.

For people who seek to live by the Word of God, such affluence poses a dilemma. How much are we allowed to enjoy it and how much of it should we give away? In a world that has given me much more than my share of its goods, how much can I keep for myself and how much should I spend on others?

Merely asking the questions sharpens our pain. The questions cannot be skirted, not if we want to hear God's Word, yet answering them is difficult. Two things are certain, in the light of biblical teaching and human experiences. First, affluence carries risks, major risks of misunderstanding and misuse; second, affluence brings obligations, weighty obligations thrust upon us by the Lord who makes affluence possible. These risks and these obligations deserve more attention than they usually receive. Understanding them may help us to live with the dilemma of our affluence even though we may not finally solve it.

The Risks of Affluence

A wise man once pondered the matter of wealth and prayed this prayer:

Two things I ask of thee;
    deny them not to me before I die:
Remove far from me falsehood and lying;
    give me neither poverty nor riches;
feed me with the food that is needful for me,
    lest I be full, and deny thee,
and say, "Who is the LORD?"
    or lest I be poor, and steal,

and profane the name of my God.
(Prov. 30:7-9)

This perceptive sage saw that one of the risks of affluence is *the risk of independence*. In his bones he felt the terror of that blasphemous question, "Who is the LORD?" It is a scornful question, equivalent to "Who needs the LORD?" It asserts that wealth alone is enough, that affluence is identical to self-sufficiency.

Seeking independence from God is both foolish and monstrous. It is foolish because there is no such thing. It is God who supplies the goods that result in wealth; it is God who gave the talent to accumulate the wealth; it is God who offers the protection to keep the wealth from being destroyed. Independence from God is monstrous because it is an idolatrous attitude. It caricatures God, wealth and the allegedly independent person: God is dwarfed into insignificance; wealth is idolized as the great benefactor and protector of humankind; the independent person is left to drift without root or anchor, heedless of his origin, careless of his purpose, mindless of his destiny. He has sneeringly asked the self-destructive question, "Who is the LORD?"

The wise man in Proverbs, with all wise people, acknowledged the risk of affluence. He begged God to save him from the ultimate temptation that affluence sets before us—the temptation to depend on it and not on God. It is appropriate that our American currency preserves the motto, "In God we trust."

A second risk of affluence is *the risk of arrogance*. It usually takes some cleverness to gain and keep more than average wealth. This cleverness may be self-deceptive: it may lead us to think that we are inherently better than those with less. We may begin to take credit where no credit is due. Did we choose the land of birth which has enabled us to have what we have? Did we choose durable genes and wise parents? When we ask such questions we realize that much of what has happened to us is not of our own doing at all. Humility is much more appropriate than arrogance in the light of all the circumstances.

James's letter to the young churches was very sensitive to the risks of wealth, especially this risk of arrogance: "Come now, you who say, 'Today or tomorrow we will go into such and such a town and spend a year there and trade and get gain'; whereas you do not know about tomorrow. What is your life? For you are a mist that appears for a little time and then vanishes. Instead you ought to say, 'If the Lord wills, we shall live and we shall do this or that.' As it is, you boast in your arrogance. All such boasting is evil" (4:13-16).

Wealth makes us feel that we are better than we are and that we control our circumstances more than we do. We who live in comfort with shelter, raiment and food in more than adequate supply need to guard against the risk of arrogance. The poor and underprivileged have enough with which to cope without being vexed by our arrogance.

The third risk of affluence is *the risk of selfishness*. The more we have, the more we think we need. Like the rich man Jesus described, some of us pull down our barns to build larger ones, ever yearning for the comfort and security that we imagine increased wealth will give. The act of acquiring becomes an endless game. "He was a fool," Jesus said. His appraisal of the situation ought to cut deep into our hearts: "So is he who lays up treasure for himself, and is not rich toward God" (Lk. 12:21).

Selfishness not only urges us to collect more than we can use, but also may lead us to abuse others in the process. James saw this happen to the wealthy around him: "Behold, the wages of the laborers who mowed your fields, which you kept back by fraud, cry out; and the cries of the harvesters have reached the ears of the Lord of hosts" (5:4).

Affluence has risks. We in our affluent countries, we who have personal affluence, must ask ourselves how well we fend off these risks. The Word of God must be our sword and shield.

The Obligations of Affluence

Affluence is both privilege and burden. Because what we gain, what we keep, what we enjoy are *God's* gifts, they bring obligations. God's gifts are always purposeful; he intends them to be used to accomplish his will.

First, affluence presses upon us *the obligation of gratitude*. Behind what we have stand the loving hands and the loving heart of God. He has owed us nothing; we have no claim to his grace. When he gives he does it freely for our good and for his service. Therefore, we can take nothing for granted. Whether we have much or little, gratitude is what we owe God. And the more we have, the more grateful we should be.

Affluence makes us more, not less, dependent on God. We need to listen to the command of the psalmist to pour out our hearts in gratefulness to the Lord and giver of life:

> Enter his gates with thanksgiving, and his courts with praise!

> Give thanks to him, bless his name!
> For the LORD is good [generous];
> > his steadfast love endures for ever,
> > and his faithfulness to all generations.
> > (Ps. 100:4-5)

Second, prosperity lays on us *the obligation of carefulness.* God has not given us the rich bounties of our lands to squander them frivolously. The wise men of Proverbs had an apt word for us:

> Precious treasure remains in a wise man's dwelling, but a foolish man devours it. (21:20)

The lesson God taught Egypt through the pharaoh's dream is important today: we need to store during times of plenty what will sustain us during times of want.

For many of us, this may mean cooking and serving less food, and ordering smaller portions in restaurants. The percentage of food wasted in the United States and Canada is horrendous. God never intended us to use our crops to spill or burn up our resources, to throw away our goods so casually. With great care he designed the universe. We are his stewards, co-rulers with him of this bountiful earth. He wants us to share his carefulness.

Finally, our wealth requires of us *the obligation of usefulness.* We are not free to use what we earn; we are not free to consume all that God gives us. We are only free to follow his purposes.

Our commitment to him, our response to his love, our reaction to Christ's death for us, our entry into the new life of the Holy Spirit—these all mean that we view wealth differently from the way we did before Christ's grace made us captive.

The example of the early church bears examination:

> Now the company of those who believed were of one heart and soul, and no one said that any of the things which he possessed was his own, but they had everything in common. And with great power the apostles gave their testimony to the resurrection of the Lord Jesus, and great grace was upon them all. There was not a needy person among them, for as many as were possessors of lands or houses sold them, and brought the proceeds of what was sold and laid it at the apostles' feet; and distribution was made to each as any had need. (Acts 4: 32-35)

We can imagine the problems that such a response would spawn today. I hope we are equally cognizant of what a burden to Christian freedom, what a barrier to Christian witness, what a hindrance to Christian mission our affluence can be.

The next time you go to the supermarket, ponder the varied brands, the multiple sizes, the lavish inventory. Let God speak to you about risks and obligations. Then do what he tells *you* to do.

For further reading

C. Freudenberger and P. Minus, Jr., *Christian Responsibility in a Hungry World*. Nashville: Abingdon, 1976.

J. Motyer, *The Day of the Lion*, Downers Grove, Ill.: IVP, 1974.

J. M. Perkins, *Let Justice Roll Down*. Glendale, Cal.: Regal, 1976.

R. Sider, ed., *Cry Justice: The Bible Speaks on Hunger and Poverty*. Downers Grove, Ill.: IVP, 1980.

R. Sider, *Rich Christians in an Age of Hunger*. Downers Grove, Ill.: IVP, 1977.

J. Yoder, *The Politics of Jesus*. Grand Rapids: Eerdmans, 1972.

Conclusion

Throughout these chapters I have assumed that we Christians: (1) can understand some of the major moral issues of human existence, (2) can apply biblical thinking to our decisions and (3) can make an essential difference to the moral character of society. This optimism apparently flies in the teeth of today's social consensus.

The seventh annual survey on "Who Runs America" contains doleful news for my kind of optimist. *U.S. News and World Report* (April 14, 1980) digested the opinions of the 1,569 leaders (in twenty-eight fields) who replied to the magazine's questionnaire. In a table titled "Institutions: Which Wield the Most Power?" organized religion ranked twenty-eight of thirty, sandwiched between the Republican Party and small business, with an average rating of about fifty per cent of that accorded The White House (ranked number one).

At least two lessons leaped from the pages of that survey: the blatantly secular outlook of the majority of the persons who were polled and the patently inadequate efforts of Christian and Jewish organizations to bear effective witness to the hope for change.

This should sober but not dishearten us. We have resources not apparent to most world opinion makers. Our passion must be to make better use of them.

Ethical insights are available. We need a firm grasp of the great realities expressed in the Scriptures: a God who is sovereign over all creation and all creatures; who is ruler of world history; who became human in Jesus; whose transforming love and power were evident in a perfect human life, a sacrificial death, a triumphant resurrection; whose presence is with and in his people through the Holy Spirit; who has formed a community to experience and display a new kind of life amid our cultures and social structures; who will come again in Jesus to complete his restoration of our world and to hold all the human family accountable for loyalty to him and his purposes.

These insights can be heightened by what we learn from God's other source of information to us, the world itself. A by-product of his creative power is that we can investigate the world. The best tools of the natural, behavioral and social sciences can contribute. Israel's wise men, especially as recounted in the book of Proverbs, looked steadily at nature and human experience, distilled their wisdom and taught their students the results. We can do something of the same when we learn from empirical investigations and studies of human behavior.

Divine forgiveness is at hand. Central to Christian morality is the confession of our constant failure to meet divine standards. We live, if we live well, not tautly anxious about our performance but humbly dependent on God's grace. Where we do succeed, it is his enablement that makes success possible; where we do not, it is his forgiveness that makes failure bearable. That amazing grace becomes the motivation for our righteousness. His unconditional love lures us to obedience.

Christian community can be counted on. We do not face our dilemmas alone. In the fellowship of other believers, knit together by the Word and the Spirit, we gain wisdom and courage to behave. We share our fears, ease our doubts, check our biases, clear our perspectives and survive our failures in the company of others who worship God and strive to live in the light of that worship.

A friend of mine had lived a totally undisciplined moral life for nearly a decade. When she finally looked hard at what had happened to her, she read her history as ten years of exploitation by the pagan selfishness of those she had called friends. "Where can I go to find help without exploitation?" was her plaintive question. She answered herself, "Back to the church." In the love and acceptance of the sons and daughters of God, she began her new life with freedom and joy.

Not a perfect company to be sure. But it is the best

available peer group to wrestle with the dilemmas that may otherwise destroy. When those around you worship the same king and seek to behave as his subjects, there will not be flawless comportment or full agreement on what comportment should be. But there will be a sensitivity to divine authority, a concern for human dignity and a hope for social transformation. That may not be the whole story; it surely, however, is much more than a good beginning.

I cannot say whether the opinion charts about Christian influence would inch up if we all took advantage of the ethical insights, divine forgiveness and Christian community which God's providence has made available. High rating in the polls is more the province of politicians and rock stars than of theologians. They need present ratings, in part at least, because they are unsure of tomorrow's destiny.

In contrast, Christ's people know to whom belong the kingdom, the power and the glory. Assured of that destiny, we can go forward with today's moral decisions—decisions which, in the midst of the ambiguities that mark our frail humanity, seek to display that kingdom, that power and that glory.